THE
Pregnant

Pause

Finding positivity when
all the results are negative.

LORI M. ALCORN

Printed in Canada by
McNally Robinson Booksellers. Grant Park.
1120 Grant Avenue. Winnipeg, Manitoba, Canada. R3M 2A6.
204-475-0483 or Toll-Free 1-800-561-1833.

ISBN 978-1-77280-240-5

Unless otherwise noted, Scripture quotations taken from The Holy Bible, New International Version® NIV® Copyright © 1973 1978 1984 2011 by Biblica, Inc. TM Used by permission. All rights reserved worldwide.

Cover Art
Watercolour art by Lori Alcorn
For font usage, thanks go to:
Selima, from JROH CREATIVE
Josefin Sans, Copyright (c) 2010, Santiago Orozco

Dedication

To my husband, my anchor,
the father of my unborn children.

I am running blind, trying to feel my way through the maze, slamming into one dead end or another, blind-sided by something, other than a wall, I am thrown to the ground and wrestling a strength I am no match for, my fear is all I have pushing me to fight, dreading how much loss will hurt, trying to prolong it as best I can.

My legs quiver.

In exhaustion and weakness.

Muscles burning.

Running on empty.

Soon they will give out.

Give up.

Eyes stinging as the tears have been depleted, have also run dry, as defeat's heated breathe can be felt on my neck, and lungs bruised from heaving, shuddering cries that slam them into my ribs, then clenching tight as the weeping robs them of air.

My lungs quiver.

In exhaustion and weakness.

Diaphragm burning.

Airways empty.

Soon they will give out.

Give up.

Battered inside and out. I am paralyzed. By the dark. By the fear. By my haggard body.

I am out of moves. I am done. Please, tell me I am done!

Count me out.

I surrender.

Prologue

~ ~ ~

Here I was again. Sitting across from a friend over coffee and dreading the inevitable question. If only skirting around talking about the issue was as easy as skirting around dealing with it. Distraction was one of my closest friends the last few months, but when sitting across from an actual friend, diversion was no longer an option. There was no hindrance to prevent her from seeing what I was hiding. Two days ago I would have had nothing to hide, as per usual. But. This was fresh pain, and without having truly faced it, it was hard to face her. I did my best to look engaged, to look her in the eyes. Then, her intuition shifted the conversation and before the question was entirely out of her mouth, I flinched. Like the prick that deflated my balloon of hope the day before, her insight released a gush of grief neither of us were prepared for.

The stress had been mounting with every month of heartbreak. The more I reached out for help the more isolated I felt. My husband withdrew and chose stoic over supportive. Didn't he know this was supposed to bring us closer together? Friends grew in distance as their families grew in number. Didn't they know I needed people to lean on more than ever? Loved ones tried to offer hope in the form of painfully ignorant guidance. Didn't they know I'd had enough 'fixing' and clearly needed empathy? God was silent and not providing any miracles. Didn't He know motherhood was the only purpose and identity I had ever felt?

It wasn't only the negative pregnancy test that broke me that day. It was also the negativity I saw in my reflection, in my fertility functions, in my attitude, in my life. My self-worth was at an all-time low and my anxiety was at an all-time high. My grief was the spark that eventually ignited a battle with depression. I felt a cold chasm expanding within my marriage, and within almost every relationship, including with God. My identity was facing a terrifyingly big, blank slate. I was losing my grip on all I held dear. There was no hiding from it anymore.

I was so tired of hiding it.

I was tired of tiptoeing around it so as not to make everyone else feel uncomfortable. Tired of the platitudes. Tired of people telling me I deserve to be a mother. Tired of people telling me I should be more desperate to be a mother. Tired of people telling me not to be desperate, I had plenty of time. I was tired of all the advice. I resented all the advice. I resented people with 'normal' fertility who had no clue. I resented my abnormal fertility. I resented my body, my age, my choices, my limitations, my doctors, my husband, my God. Everything.

And I was tired of resenting everything.

I was so tired of it all.

I wanted to let go.

Only four years in and I was done. I had been through all the tests, with all the results coming up negative, just like my pregnancy tests. What started as a journey towards a bundle of joy ended up the most heartbreaking road I'd ever walked. What started as the ultimate union between husband and wife ended up creating the widest rift we'd ever encountered. The future I hoped for was decomposing before my eyes, and the decay was now eating away at the present. It made me feel like my whole life was rotten. I could see it, like gangrene's voracious appetite for healthy, living tissue, this negativity wanted to devour everything that was still vibrant and valuable about my life. I knew I needed to stop the spread before it consumed my life. Before it consumed me.

I wanted to let it go.

I had to let it go.

But how? The only dream I'd ever had was being dismantled, how could I find another? Why me? What now? How do I get back to that joy-filled, hopeful, positive person I used to be? Where do I even begin?

And so those are the questions I spent the next several years trying to figure out. I needed to figure out how to let go so I could receive something new.

And so I did.

And that's why I am sharing my story with you, for those who are unsure of their own story in the pause.

Thirteen years in and my story isn't the typical miracle or happy ending. My story isn't going through whatever treatments it takes to get the family we want. My story isn't growing a family through adoption or fostering. My family of two still feels unfinished and we weren't satisfied choosing a child-free life. My story is about what it's like to live with no answers, no next steps, no idea what is in store for my family. And it could have been about having no hope.

But it isn't.

I am here to let you know, if you find yourself drowning in negativity, there is a path to positivity through it all. There is a joy-filled life still awaiting you. I would love it if you would join me on this journey. My journey to becoming positive, when all the results are negative.

Chapter one

"It is not a slight thing when those so fresh from God love us."
~ Charles Dickens

~ ~ ~

For me, holding a baby erases all doubt that there is a God. If there was ever proof of the miraculous, a tiny little life is it. To be able to have in my arms something so recently in His presence, it is a slice of Heaven.

Since a very young age I have considered myself a baby whisperer, from a family full of baby whisperers. We were the ones sure to be found holding any baby in the vicinity, so I was a baby-sitter from the earliest age possible and at every opportunity. Where a baby was crying inconsolably, I would swoop in to sooth, un-phased by the demanding decibels. I loved the challenge of entertaining a testy or timid toddler, and savoured the squeals of laughter I inevitably induced. I could watch them for hours; sleeping, playing, learning, every part of their little lives brought me joy.

The moment I was holding a baby or playing with a child, my heart felt something incredibly special. I would be flooded with warmth and affection, even if I barely knew the child or its family. My heart opened wide and love simultaneously poured in and out at the same time. I have often wondered if they can tell how much I love them because they always seem to love me back. As long as I can remember, I have considered babies the world's greatest miracles.

In the family I grew up in, this affinity for caregiving and nurturing wasn't anything noteworthy, it was the norm. I saw it in my mom, my cousins, my sisters, it was all around me. It wasn't my special skills that made motherhood my calling, to me it was the children that were special. I wanted to feel that bond always. It wasn't until much later in life that I felt it was my one true calling.

Early on, my calling to motherhood was part of the plan, but as a child I was full of dreams. These changed about as frequently as the next new creative endeavor I was introduced to. Hair dresser, painter, author, journalist, photographer, fashion designer, architect, interior designer, advertising, and the list goes on. As a teenager, I wiled away the hours sketching, painting, colouring, crafting, and playing with pretty much any art medium I could get my hands on. I hadn't decided on a career yet, all I knew was that I wanted to do something creative.

If you had asked me then what I thought about my identity, I likely would have assumed I knew myself. Considering how fast my interests would change, it is no wonder that I in fact didn't. I know now, in hindsight, what a late bloomer I actually was. I was so unsure of myself. I knew what I liked to do but I didn't feel I was talented enough at those things. Besides, some of my best giftings had not even begun to grow yet.

Even while I was on the cusp of making what I thought were lifelong adult decisions, I didn't have a hot clue about my purpose. Besides that, encouragement was sparse while competition was fierce in high school. And that was only in my little town of 10,000. Every time I explored a passion I became daunted at how much rivalry would be out there in the 'real world'. This was what our grade 12 teachers were frequently reminding us of, in attempts to prepare us for the inevitable. Soon my dreams were just another thing to fear.

~ | | ~

Fear and I were old friends by the time I reached eighteen. I say friends because it was a relationship not unlike many of my others over the course of my youth, where I buried my needs and went along with whatever others wanted. My fear and my friends dominated most of my decisions, since I mistook my need for extroversion for a need to be liked by everyone. My personal value greatly depended on the validation I received when others liked me. I did whatever it took not to rock the boat, to keep their appreciation for me as status quo, and to keep myself within the social circle that I craved. In my mid-30's I learned that this is called co-dependence. There were many reasons I had grown to be co-dependent, some of them nature, some of them nurture. But the 'why' didn't matter at the time because fixing it wasn't even on the radar. The only thing that was? Being loved.

Now that did have a lot to do with my nature. Again, because I was a late bloomer, these are all revelations I had when I was much closer to middle-aged than to middle school. I can see now that I was a child obsessed with feeling loved, because I was a child who felt deeply. And if you feel things deeply, it would be nice if they were predominately good feelings. Not only did I yearn to feel that love directed toward me, but I also longed to pour out the love I felt on others.

During my teen years I heard a saying which I adopted as my own personal motto, it was, "Love and be loved." I thought my existence began and ended with love. I wasn't wholly wrong, but I wasn't exactly right either. When I loved, I loved whole-heartedly, frequently with very little reason to, and therefore giving much more than I ever received. And my default of feeling things deeply made every word someone spoke to me that much more personal, positively or negatively. This made for some very deep heartache, as I was often crushed by crushes who didn't like me as much as their words had implied, or who let me down harshly. Friendships didn't fare much better.

Because this was my nature from a very early age, I had quite the collection of wounds by the time I graduated high school, none of them sufficiently healed. I gradually began to try less and with less people, my way of connecting to people was not sustainable. Of course, this led to being actually alone, instead of just feeling lonely. In my loneliness, I turned to an internal, invented world, where I could imagine the perfect existence. It offered me something that real world relationships couldn't seem to be able to offer me. For a variety of reasons, I identified that as a romantic relationship. *That* would hold the key to true acceptance, I thought. So I began to build a fantasy life with the guy who would love me as I am. I envisioned that he would know exactly who that was, even if I didn't. I played out all the ways I would be able to love on him. And, of course, our children. I lived in this fictional fairy-tale, hoping that somehow, one day, 'my prince would come.' He would come and he would make it all come true.

~ | | ~

I was 22 when I finally met my prince, and as the saying goes, 'but I kissed a lot of frogs first'. Well, not exactly.

I only got to the kissing stage with two, and by the time I met him I no longer believed in princes anyway, however that is a different story for another time. In the four years of adulting that it took to meet him, I had become even more convinced my aspirations of being in any creative industry were delusional dreams of grandeur. Dreams I needed to pack away with the rest of my childhood things.

At age 19 I left for the city, determined not to end up in the small town jobs that trapped the uneducated. I may not have known what I wanted to do as a career anymore, but I knew the city had to have better options. Over the next several years, the women I worked with unintentionally gave the unified impression I had a lot of time to wait for children, so I continued to try to figure out my 'for now' career. And like I said, three years later, I had come to the conclusion I was simply going to work at something where my skills at being average and ordinary could pay the bills. That was until I met Mr. Right and I could be the stay at home mom I had now made my number one dream.

As much as I was determined to become a mother, I was correspondingly resolved to have a solid marriage before children. As much as I wanted children, to me they were only a product of love, I would not be settling for one without the other. I was convinced, and stayed convinced, for the next six years, that my plan for timing was just fine. Considering my family history with fertility, I could have been more concerned, but somehow I wasn't. I grew increasingly convinced that children were my one path to true fulfillment, and because of my certainty I was willing to defer it, to do it right.

During that time I still enjoyed many creative hobbies, but that is all they were. They were something on the side to keep me occupied until they could fit into the future I was waiting for. In fact, many of them I began seeing as fulfilling when I combined them with motherhood. When I had a creative inspiration, the kind I previously tried to translate into making a living, I adapted it into a hobby. It was even better if it was something I could one day do during the naps of little ones, or as a homeschooling project. I had devised the perfect plan, I thought. It was the best of both worlds. Being a stay at home mom would bring the freedom for whatever creative outlets I wanted to pursue. All without the pressure of having to make a living with my creations.

To a degree, this helped with my patience as I waited. Of course, only for a time, because I didn't yet realize how much of my personality was purpose driven. I yearned to have a purpose. Over the years I began to feel empty and hopeless when I didn't have that thing that told me my life had meaning. Yet, for all my searching, nothing dissuaded me from my belief that I only had the one purpose. It may have started out that I wanted motherhood because of my love for children, but ultimately it formed into my life's meaning. I realized so many of my strengths lay in being a nurturer, and not only was this one of my greatest passions, but for once I found an area of life that I didn't fear competition. I had found my confidence.

~ | | ~

So back to prince charming. He was no prince, more of a knight in shining armor type, but he certainly was charming. If he could have, my cowboy wanna-be would have rode in on his trusty steed and swept me off my feet, rescuing me. He was a rescuer and I was a girl who needed rescuing. From herself.

The road to falling in love was paved with... no, scratch that, that implies it was smooth. It was anything but smooth. It was the kind of roads we drive on here where we live, in Winnipeg, Manitoba. They are full of potholes and uneven surfaces that leave you jostled and frustrated, even with the best of shocks. But while the road was not easy, we were. We had something instant, and I wouldn't call it chemistry, it was deeper and more meaningful than that. We shared so much, from our core values to our specific brand of humor, and so falling in love was easy. This was the first relationship in my life, the first anything in my life, that truly felt 'meant to be.'

We were easy, but we were also young. He even younger than I, by three years. So I was very patient with timelines, I didn't push him to get married. And once we did, I agreed to his request to wait five years to have children, when I would be 30 and he would be 27. This all seemed very reasonable and smart, in the moment. It's likely that's because I was convinced now that I had found love, my life was unfolding perfectly, exactly the way I'd hoped. To me that meant I could finally relax, the desperation for love and purpose was finished. But the unfolding was merely the beginning of the unraveling.

chapter ll one

Chapter two

"Life is full of surprises. Why is that always surprising." ~
Cathleen Schine

~ ~ ~

Life is full of surprises. Surprises that unexpectedly and
utterly change the trajectory of your life. Falling in love
with my husband was one of those surprises, falling so
instantly and intensely. An immediate bond. And then it
happened again. I was completely caught off guard.

It likely began months before that moment actually
happened, but it only took one second for my whole
being to know undoubtedly. I had only been holding my
first niece for that one second when I already knew I had
a bond with her that nothing would ever break. It went
beyond that Heavenly moment I have with all babies. It
was deeper than the skin that would one day look akin to
mine, or our blood that connected us for life. It was
something else. Once again, falling so instantly and
intensely in love. My breath caught in my throat as I

tried to express the inexpressible, the overwhelming feelings swelling within me. But all I could do was smile and choke back the tears. She wasn't even my own child and yet the force of my love for her told me I was never going to see the world the same way again. I thought I had been certain I was meant to be a mom before that moment, but now it was cemented. My desire multiplied by a million.

It was now a few months shy of two years before I hit the big 3-0. I had been patient, but for the first time since we were married, I wanted to push up the baby-making timeline with my husband. All my plans to wait another two years before holding my own miracle flew out the window then. Though I didn't act on that impulse immediately. Like most people falling in love I harbored my feelings, contemplating them, trying to see if they were 'right'. And also, like someone falling in love, I couldn't stay away from the object of my affection.

I wanted to see her as often as possible. I wanted to stare into her beautiful eyes, and have her stare back into mine. I wanted to caress her soft hands, kiss her chubby cheeks, and hold her for hours. I had some extra vacation time that hubby didn't, so I took off that first week home from the hospital to help her mom. My middle sister hadn't been as much of a babysitter as I, so I knew she would need some support. And I could soak in all the aunty time I wanted. The hours I spent in the car, driving to and from my home town, ended up time I spent practicing my speech. I layered in all the reasons why we shouldn't wait into my ironclad arguments, anticipating all the angles. I wanted to be sure to win hubby over with my logic, as much as my heart.

~ | | ~

Work was getting very stressful, and it made me contemplate that I may be getting a sign it was time to move on to the next phase of my career, motherhood. I was making too much money to quit, or look somewhere else, but maternity benefits would be very generous. He also had a well-paying job so we were financially much better off than anticipated, when we first decided we would start trying summer of 2007. We owned a house that had enough room for us and a child, we had a reliable vehicle with room for kids, and we had much more stability than most people before beginning a family.

It had also recently occurred to me that at that moment I was the age my mom was when she had me, and it took her five years to get pregnant. This is when the family fertility history grew as a concern, as I also had two other aunts with fertility issues as well. If we didn't start now we may not have children until I was much older than I wanted to be, or we may not be able to have kids at all. I was already noticing how much I was feeling my age physically, due to excess weight, and I was beginning to have similar symptoms my mom was experiencing. How would I manage in a few years with my own children?

And that was another thing, my parents health was also something I was increasingly concerned about. My dad, less than a month from 60, and who had high blood pressure and cholesterol issues for decades, was now also having chest pains occasionally. That year he had also been diagnosed with the type 2 diabetes, which runs rampant in our family. And Mom's hip problem, the one I had inherited from her already, was getting worse, with talk of her needing it replaced. Of course this ends up as a wake-up call that my parents are mortal and won't always be around, and I'd like to give them as many years with our children as possible.

With all these thoughts overloading my mind, a few weeks later, I finally talked to my husband about the possibility of starting our family early. There was no room in my mind, or heart, for the answer to be no. How could I wait one second longer to have a child myself? But that was it, I couldn't do it by myself. That's not what marriage is about, we were one, even when we wanted different things. This was my husband's life, and these were his children too, as much as mine, and we needed to be on the same page. However, after much deliberation on his part, approximately seven excruciating days, the answer came back yes!

~ 11 ~

Two months later, when the birth control ran out, and two months shy of our third anniversary, we were officially trying to conceive. Or as hubby liked to call it, 'stopped interrupting nature.' Now, this officiality only extended to the inhabitants of our home, me and him. We were ready to start trying to bring a baby into the world, we were not ready for all the questions and advice likely to come with broadcasting the news. Even though I had received a yes, he was hoping it wouldn't happen immediately, and was still worried he wasn't going to be a good father. He was happy to avoid the attention on this new development for a little while longer.

It was incredibly hard to keep this secret, especially one so exciting. I was thrilled and wanted to do a happy dance with someone, anyone! Especially since I wasn't about to find a dance partner in my husband, this was a compromise not a celebration. But I was determined to be completely respectful of his needs during this journey, I was just happy to be on it! Of course, he wasn't the only one compromising. Because he was at the shallow end, only dipping his toe in the pool so to speak, I had to reign in my desire to dive into the deep end. Especially since I had long been preparing for this day.

I've often said I should have been a girl scout because I am always prepared. By nature I am a planner and researcher, so long before we had moved up our baby-making schedule, I had done much investigating into what trying to conceive should entail. Fifteen years after the internet became mainstream it seemed like I had all the information I could ever need. I knew how to determine ovulation through temperature tracking. I knew based on my cycle approximately when that should be. I knew that it can take several months for birth control hormones to leave your system. I was certain I was anything but ignorant, I was as informed as anyone I knew, and more in most cases.

I was also ready with research on how we could conceivably enhance the conception process, but I was also still resolved that our children would be the product of love only. I had to balance that with his uneasiness with charting, regulated types of underwear to wear, or meeting love making quotas, or any other baby-factory-like production mechanics. So I started simple and small.

I began taking prenatal vitamins, taking my temperature, and keeping a tracking journal, after all, I had to feel like I was doing something! It is a good thing I was well aware that it was normal not to get pregnant in the first year of trying. After being on birth control for so many years I knew there was no point into rushing into all the other typical 'trying to conceive' methods right then anyway. Compromise can be a lot easier when there are other factors influencing the situation. In this case, my understanding of those biological factors were a big help in enhancing my patience.

These baby steps that inched us along also gave me the opportunity to work on convincing my husband what a great father he'd be. As much as I wanted children, I wanted him to want it too. As I mentioned already, all along it was about creating a family, just as much as it was about my own desire to mother. But because he didn't grow up with a good example of a marriage or a father, I knew he was still dealing with the emotional fallout from that. The last thing he wanted to do was raise children in that cycle, since he wasn't certain he could escape his father's patterns. I loved him all the more for being more concerned with the wellness of our potential children than fulfilling our desires. Sure, fear was part of his reasoning, but I knew his heart was in the right place, wanting the best for our children. Even at the expense of ourselves. How could I be anything but supportive of that?

~ | | ~

Despite my toned-down attempts of trying to improve our odds, and my imperfect knowledge of biology, it wasn't even a full year before I had grown quite discouraged. Somehow the information I had on ovulation tracking wasn't as precise as I needed, and I grew frustrated with all the methods I tried. It didn't help that my cycle wasn't stable yet. Maybe if I had just ignored all those tempting tools I found online I wouldn't have had so many measures to be disappointed by, but living out the first year of 'trying to conceive' in ignorance just wasn't me. For me, ignorance was rarely bliss. I almost always knew there had to be more information somewhere, part of my 'always be prepared' default I suppose.

Seven months in I learned the lesson that five days late might mean nothing, especially when cycles still haven't found their rhythm. Eight months in I learned even seven days doesn't necessarily mean anything. Other signs pointed to the possibility of a miscarriage, but doctors frown at that word and prefer terminology like 'it wasn't a viable pregnancy.' It didn't need to be labelled for me to feel profound loss and sadness though. My first taste of real grief.

The fact that trying was still a secret wasn't the only reason I sank into a silence. The internal noise of pain, confusion, loss, grief, and uncertainty, all rattling around my brain were enough to deal with. I did share my suspicions with hubby, who had never been good with words when I was distraught, and so he tried to fix it with a Dairy Queen blizzard. Not that I minded, but after years of trying to fix my feelings with ice cream, I knew it wouldn't last.   I was aching for his arms or acknowledgement. But I was too caught up in trying to not to seem so needy, and he was not equipped to express the emotions I needed back then.

The next week was so very hard to get through. Every friend I encountered I wanted to blurt out all the pain I had pent up inside. It was full to the brim and ready to spill over at any moment. I don't believe it was a coincidence when my sister reached out for a lunch date that week, on a day she had some extra time between her classes. My baby sister, five years my junior but already so ahead of me in many ways.

As it turns out, she had been ahead of me in the 'trying to have a baby department' as well, by half a year. We had both been keeping the same secret for all these months, and it was a secret that was bound and determined to see the light of day that afternoon. Finally, I had someone to not only tell, but share everything I'd experienced on this journey. Everything I mentioned she had also felt, feared, and fretted over. We were no longer alone, not only in the trying, but in the difficulties of trying as well.

Up until that moment, I had only known two acquaintances that weren't able to have children. They both seemed to have had the fortune of finding their path early on, one adopted and one chose the child-free life. While I only had a slight inclination at the time of where my motherhood journey was leading me, I had become very aware of how isolated the experience would be. To have that suddenly reversed, and to be able to walk this with my sister of all people, was a great surprise and of great comfort to me.

~ | | ~

We were eleven months into our endeavour to expand our family when my middle sister was giving birth to her second sweet baby girl, and we hit our next big obstacle. It started off as the pursuit of a real encounter with God, a chance to strengthen our connection to Him. While it did accomplish that, it also unpacked a lot of baggage for us both. We were able to unburden the shame that had clung to us for far too long. For him, it was about those father issues, and for me, it was my life long anxiety as well as the abusive relationship my fear and codependence had got me into.

It's never easy to face our greatest shame, but we were immediately thankful we had taken that step. We knew it would make us better parents, and of course, better people. Of course healing was not a one and done situation, it ended up being an eight month detour from our focused fertility efforts. At one point I realized the stress my mental, emotional, and spiritual well-being were placing on my body, and that it could be related to our inability to conceive. Would there be ripple effects of healing on my body through this spiritual healing as well?

Another fairly significant insight also occurred to me during this time. One of my goals was to share my whole journey, with my children one day. The good, the bad and the ugly. My hope was that they wouldn't repeat my mistakes if I shared my consequences. Yet, I had not been willing to share it with most everyone else in my life. How could I expect them to learn those lessons as long as I held on to my secrets? Maybe that was another part of the block to our fertility? Regardless, I decided that I was going to embark on a truth mission, to become an open book about my past. I was no longer going to be afraid of being vulnerable, no longer hiding behind shame.

Between working on all that, I was also on to a new job, and the only thing I had time for in the reproduction department was my continued effort to lose weight. This diversion was actually quite a nice break from thinking about trying to get pregnant all the time. A break from being consumed with the lack of control, the heartache, the impatience. Right before this hurdle, I had been chomping at the bit, ready to go to any lengths for a baby. No matter how much it stretched our marital tie that binds. It was beginning to pull so hard that it was bound to snap at any moment, if I hadn't been pulled in this other direction.

This unofficial interruption from trying helped refocus me, and it was through these revelations that I realized I was not in control, only God was. Only God could remove any of the barriers that found their way into our path. And they would be removed only if and when He wanted to remove them. It may be a doctor, or a pill, or timing, but whatever it might be that would bring us children, it was still only because of God's will, not mine. That didn't mean we didn't have a role to play, there were still steps we could take to open doors, but then it was up to God if they stayed open or became closed.

Nineteen months into our journey, I called up the doctor's office to make an appointment to talk about our difficulties getting pregnant, to see if this direction would be our open door.

Chapter three

"After 30, a body has a mind of its own." ~ Bette Midler

~ ~ ~

I already had my "Ahhh! I'm almost 30!" freak-out two years before the actual birthday, so when my champagne birthday came along I was already ok with that age in general. I had, however, now crossed that invisible age line where suddenly things become more challenging and risky. Not by a large percent, but large enough to give pause.

I had a doctor's appointment in early December that year, to finally talk getting a referral to a fertility specialist. As it turned out, I was eight days late on the day of my appointment. Hope was beginning to take the wheel again, and the uninformed things people say, like, 'it always happens when you....' reverberated through my mind. I wondered, is it happening now that I've experienced so much emotional healing? Is it happening now that I've taken steps to get help? I took a pregnancy test, which was once again negative, wondering why did I always do that to myself? Four days later I had my referral letter for the local fertility clinic....and I also had my period. Twelve days late. This was the latest I had been so far. With Christmas a few weeks away, I had already imagined being able to surprise my whole family at our gathering with some silly gift announcement. And nine months down the road would be so close to my birthday, what a perfect gift that would be. Would have been. Hope once again steered me wrong, and almost off of a cliff.

The pain and bitterness had not subsided by Christmas so I was working hard to take solace in my love for the Christmas season. I tried to focus on the gratitude of being with my family and my precious nieces, doing my best not to think about what might have been. It was actually working until the moment my middle sister announced she was pregnant again, with her third child. She also felt the need to state it was her last child, and that if I, or our youngest sister, wanted to be able to have a child close in age to hers, we had only until March to get pregnant.

Really.

As if a deadline was just what we needed. As if it was completely within our control. Because that had proven to be true so far. At this point, it was no longer a secret in our family, my sister and I had revealed some time ago that we had both been trying without success. The obliviousness wasn't because she wasn't aware of the situation, no, she was only unaware of our grief. Unaware of how painful the struggle to get pregnant was for us. Unaware of how complicated the process was for us. As if we simply hadn't tried hard enough yet. Or up until now, it must not have been that important to us. One could only assume what she had assumed.

The specifics of our situation seemed somehow lost on the mom-to-be. And I just about lost it on her. It took all my strength not to start crying and tell her that a mere two weeks ago I had lost my baby. I hadn't been 100% certain of that, but it most certainly could have been true! But I mostly just wanted to lash out, to open her eyes to how hurtful her words were. She lived in a world where getting pregnant had happened 3 times in 3 years, fertility was something she could speak about flippantly. She had no reason to put two and two together, to see it wasn't that easy at all for us two. We weren't sure how she could have missed pain multiplied by two, but she did. The saddest part was that it took all the joy away from the fact were going to be aunties once again.

~ | | ~

Finally, in March, days after our fifth anniversary, we had our first appointment with the specialist. I was asked all the questions I anticipated we would be, after all, I was still doing my research. Then came the generic tips, are we doing this, are we doing that. Five years in the future I would be given a book, written in 1995, which blew my mind, and blew this doctor's knowledge out of the water. Simple things this fertility specialist should have known by 2008! Simple things he shared incorrectly or didn't share at all but should have.

Simple things like I needed a thermometer with decimal places. He didn't even question my unsuccessful temperature readings, which were due to a thermometer that couldn't detect the minuscule fluctuations I would need to see. I said I had given up on ovulation tracking because I wasn't seeing what I needed to make a determination, so he said, "well, just stick to day 14 then." Well, even at that time, I knew enough that those numbers didn't add up, my cycle was anywhere from 31 to 35 days long. That was my first clue this specialist wasn't as specialized as he claimed to be.

We then went through our first rounds of testing, and of course, all the tests came back negative. We once again sat down with the doctor to review the results, where he explained all of our results were negative, meaning they were within normal parameters. Usually when you are going through medical testing, it is anything but positive to hear "you've tested positive for....", but at least it would have meant one step closer to a solution. He offered to send me for a few more tests, a deeper dive figuratively and literally, which I took him up on. In the meantime he offered his best speculation, my weight was interfering with my insulin levels, which in turn interfered with the estrogen my body should produce to release an egg. Even though the blood tests for estrogen came back normal, because of my weight, he still thought it might be the issue. My long cycles indicated a delayed ovulation, in turn making it difficult to know when to time 'reproduction activities.' An admittance the 14-day ovulation was wrong? Not one he formally acknowledged anyway. Then, he proceeded to encourage natural weight loss, as well as investing in ovulation tests, then sent me on my way with a prescription to regulate my insulin. And the promise of future testing appointments to follow.

~ | | ~

At first I was thrilled it could be that simple, maybe we wouldn't even need the other tests! In the moment, I looked at my husband to see if he was ok with this step, to which he nodded. We were now much further along than simply 'not interrupting nature', but we weren't yet ready for fully manipulating nature either. This felt like a small and simple step we could manage. A few days later I already had the medication, which didn't even break the bank. This was a bonus for us because another thing on our list of 'what not to do to have a baby,' was go into debt.

However, it was only two months later, two more negative tests, and two souls doing some searching, when we decided the medication was not for us after all. Or rather me. For one thing, it was making me nauseous, not a good symptom when you are hoping for morning sickness. We also realized the drugs were tricking my body to think it was healthy enough to produce the right amount of estrogen when in fact we didn't even know if my body needed tricking. We wondered how would we know when my weight loss allowed my body to correct itself and when to stop the medication. Especially since the doctor outright said I wouldn't know what the magic number on the scale would be to fix my estrogen. I had been in such a rush to believe the pills could be my quick fix, we didn't take time to really think it through. But once we had, we decided it was no longer an option at all.

At first, it was pretty hard to let go of that illusion of control. It made sense to quit trying to artificially make my body do something if I could do it in a healthy way, but I felt like it was letting go of all the control. Somehow, the idea I had any control had crept back into my mind. I also knew I was still in control of losing weight, but it wasn't the same, it didn't feel as tangible as the medication. Not that I was truly in control of whether the pills worked either, it just felt a whole lot more comfortable when we had a course of action.

My husband on the other hand liked not being in control. He was of the opinion he would be braver about being a father if God was to give us a child naturally, like a vote of confidence from God. With any option that would increase the manipulation of nature, so did his unwillingness to try that option.

We quickly realized we would have to discuss in great lengths what lengths we were willing to go to in order to become parents. Turns out we disagreed on many of the finer points of assisted trying to conceive. However, after weeks of discussing, the bottom line was that we both were certain we didn't like any of the choices we were given. We didn't have enough information about any other alternatives, so we tried the 'wait and see' option. Yet, with every passing month I once again switched back on to that track of dogged determination in making it happen. I of course began doing what I do best, which is research. I began talking about fertility challenges with others, asking questions, and hunting for clues on the internet. I followed every lead like a blood hound who was hot on a scent, relentless in finding an answer.

In the meantime, everything collectively took a heavy toll on my body, heart and mind. There came a point there was no longer a reason to go back to see any doctors, every test was negative, and every option was a 'no'. But I was still trapped in the waiting room of my pregnant pause, waiting for my bundle of joy to arrive.

~ | | ~

Three and a half years in and I was so very tired of feeling alone in the waiting. By now even my baby sister was finally pregnant. After four years of trying they had made the decision to move to the adoption option instead, and then she found herself in the middle of a miracle. I was beyond ecstatic for her, a reminder miracles do still happen! My hope bounced back a little in that moment and it was nice to feel some positivity in my life once again. Yet, my one bona fide partner in this pain was now free of it. She of course still understood, but it felt wrong to want to keep talking about it with her when she now was able to move forward. Why make her look back?

I knew I had many supportive people surrounding me, more than a lot of other women I knew, but supportive was different than understanding. My middle sister became much more sensitive after I talked to her openly about how her 'encouraging' words were actually wounding me, but it still wasn't like talking to someone who knew first hand. And even though my parents had their own years of not being able to get pregnant, and I assumed they would be more empathetic, they instead focused more on offering suggestions to fix it. It became a topic I learned to avoid all together, so as to avoid the messy feelings that came with it.

It wasn't only family, a lot of people didn't get what I was going through, which isn't in itself bad, it was just bad for me. People not knowing how to respond, making for awkward or painful conversations. People would assume I was feeling a particular way, but I was often feeling any number of things. People would assume I would naturally follow their idea of the 'usual' path and didn't understand when it wasn't for us. So instead, I avoided sharing anything to do with what was happening in the pause. And that was bad for me too.

I decided to try looking online for forums or groups that dealt with fertility struggles, to find some connection and belonging to people more like me. People who understood that it's as much what to say as what not to say. It was a strange new world, like its own culture, a culture full of its own language and even 'regional' dialects. There seemed to be quite distinct camps depending on the path each person decided to take. There also seemed to be a slight hostility to those from other camps which I could never understand. Not to mention the overt hostility towards baby-bearers that I unfortunately did understand, but was trying very hard to relinquish. Ultimately I found it was hard to identify with anyone because of these alliances, as I myself did not have a path yet. I was fairly certain 90% of their camps I would never belong to. And once again I found myself feeling alone, even in my own so-called tribe.

~ | | ~

So it happened once again. I found myself begin to intensely internalize, getting stuck in my own mind. Only having conversations with myself about all that was going on. Hoping alone. Taking the pregnancy tests alone. Grieving alone. Every time I wallowed in disappointment, the same questions would run through my mind. If there are no answers to my fertility issues, how will I know when to stop hoping? I was getting no answers from doctors and no answers from God. There wasn't a 'you will never' or 'one day you will.' Would there ever be a concrete yes or no? When should I accept there is no longer a chance? And most of all, how would I survive the limbo until that was figured out?

I felt like I was hoping too much for something which I was never promised. Yet, wasn't I made for this? Without a clear 'no', could I ever truly give up? It was being neither here nor there that was driving me crazy. I was feeling like I was standing with my feet on two paths, two paths in opposite directions. Because it is almost impossible for my legs to go in both directions, I was unable to move forward from that position. I was going nowhere.

I was also secretly harboring a thought I couldn't yet verbalize. I was seriously considering the idea I would never be a parent. In order to be realistic, I had to at least admit it was possible. Every day it was more and more possible. And more and more likely. However, the fact I was beginning to doubt must have been leaking out and people were catching on. Increasingly I was hearing people tell me of stories of people they knew getting pregnant after five, seven, even ten years of trying. Or telling me new options they thought I may not have heard of yet. Or telling me three years was too early to give up hope.

They obviously had no idea how hard it was to hold on to hope for that long, with no break. Like when lifting weights, during the lifting or releasing, or shifting, the weight is manageable. But try just holding that weight, arms out, and quickly that weight feels like it's multiplying its burden by the second. The same can be said for hope. When there is no movement being made, hope can be tremendously weighty.

When faced with the direct question one day, "You are not giving up are you?" my answer was "No," but I continued, "however, I also don't want live in denial that being barren is a possibility." I felt like I was the only one living in reality, the only one who didn't see it as black and white, full of easy answers and one-size fits all options. This was my path, no one else's, and I had to figure out the balance between faith, hope and realism until the waiting was over.

~ | | ~

Somehow, the monotony of constantly monitoring my cycle made time both crawl and fly. Then, suddenly one day I was counting, and it had been forty-eight cycles of disappointment. Four possible miscarriages, five negative pregnancy tests, six negative fertility tests. The planner in me had anticipated a few small bumps in the road, while awaiting the big baby bump, and as much as I tried to prepare for the almost certain minor detours, nothing prepared us for the journey we ended up on.

I was getting worn down by the discouragement of hitting a wall of constant 'nos', of receiving negative results over and over. I was falling into a depression over being denied my dreams. I was feeling the division in my marriage as we both crawled within ourselves to hash out our failures. After four years of this pregnant pause, and the painful labor of merely trying, I became determined joy had to come in other shapes than a baby, and that trying to expand love shouldn't divide it.

I found my breaking point on an ordinary day, in the middle of the week, after work in the midst of getting supper ready. Though it was too early to 'feel' anything, I sure felt horribly empty after the fact. It was the seventh day late when my period came after all, that gravely empty chasm within was so expansive, I thought I'd flushed my heart too. And I was suddenly so done with that feeling. It didn't take more than a few seconds of feeling that intense ache radiating through my womb to the rest of my body, before I flushed my dreams too. I washed my hands of it. Once again, I wasn't certain a life had ended that day, but death was certainly hovering, and I felt like if I didn't choose the choice would be made for me. Or worse, it would be an 'all of the above' type situation. I had to let my dream of being a mother die, before my marriage did, or my spirit. They were both being consumed by the hunger of the void, the black hole I called my empty womb.

I walked immediately into the living room where my husband watched t.v., oblivious to the carnage, and matter-of-factly stated I was completely done with trying to get pregnant. I had made up my mind, my hope balloon had burst for the last time. It had been overinflated, stretched so far to the point it had to float or pop.

It always popped.

And now I was the one deflated.

Chapter four

"Search me, God, and know my heart, test me and know my anxious thoughts."~ Psalm 139:23

~ ~ ~

Fears, or anxiousness, whatever you want to name my ever growing list of reasons I was becoming more ok with not having children, I was torn about allowing these to continue. I wanted to let them continue in case they were meant to bring me some comfort and peace about being childless. I didn't want to let them continue in case they were unhelpful thoughts I should have been taking captive, trying not be anxious about anything. It was difficult to know whether I was supposed to be 'facing facts' or 'holding on to hope'.

I had yet to experience any tangible answers, but when I started following the blog of another infertility journey, her words jumped right off the screen and landed deep within my heart. "I believe God can do miracles, but I am finding it hard to believe he will choose to do it for us.

Something in me is telling me that my body is just not going to let this happen. I don't know if it's my own pessimism, the enemy, or the Holy Spirit. I don't know whether to believe it or refute it. I wish we just knew one way or the other. I need some black and white. I need a plan, all this grey, and all this "wait and see" feels like such a heavy burden on our shoulders.... I am left desperate for hope. Real hope - and a little perspective." My entire being screamed, "Me too!" Was I supposed to be ok with the way things were? Were my anxious thoughts not my own? Was the idea to 'let go' the comforting whisper of the Holy Spirit?

It wasn't long before I began throwing around new terms and new outlooks to help me figure out where I was truly at. Did I want to completely give up on the idea of having children? No, of course not. But I began to believe the only way I would have children would be a miracle. Now I still believed every baby was a miracle, and maybe even more so now. Now that I knew the average odds of conception actually resulting in the birth of a healthy baby were fairly low. But for myself, I knew then our baby would have to be a *supernatural* miracle. And that led me to finally label myself infertile. This wasn't the first time I had thrown around the term infertility, but it was the first time I owned it. So I am infertile, now what?

Infertility is like getting fired from the job of motherhood. You build up a fantastic resume of expertise, talent, knowledge, and all the things that would make you an excellent 'employee.' You get hired as a trainee, working hard toward that final project that will get you permanently hired, but that project just somehow keeps failing. Nothing that you've tried works. And so 'they' tell you, they are freeing up your future by pointing you in another direction. The door. Some may be able to immediately pick themselves up, brush themselves off, move on, and begin working towards a new future. But what if that job was all you ever wanted? The only job you could see providing a fulfilling future? Suddenly your, old 'co-workers' are hard to be around or they don't *want* to be around. Pointing fingers is a waste of time. All those skills are no longer necessary and you don't know what to do with yourself. All you can ask is, 'what now?!'

Well, now I had to discover what I was going to do for the rest of my life, that's what. In addition to a supernatural pregnancy, I was also hoping for a supernatural revelation of my purpose. What else was I created for? I didn't exactly get the answer I was hoping for, but I did get reassurance. It came from a teaching one Sunday morning at church, and led to a huge light-bulb moment for me.

Everyone leaves a legacy. My actions would leave something behind, with or without having biological children. The time had come to realize that the plan I was designed for was already in play. I hadn't been chasing God's dream, I had been chasing my own. And His plans for me would be the same with or without me giving birth. My purpose is my purpose and that would never change, because parenthood was a circumstance not a destiny. I still didn't know for sure whether children played a part in my purpose or not, but I knew if I had been a mother that morning, in that moment of insight, I might have continued to be blinded to where God was trying to lead me next. I wouldn't have been searching, heart and eyes open, waiting, expecting something new from Him.

~ | | ~

I used to think that the phrase, 'I need to find myself' was a silly and self-indulgent notion. I felt that self-discovery was a much more appropriate and healthy way of approaching growth and maturation. But that was before I had ever really felt lost. I may have felt lonely or lacking but never lost. It wasn't until several years later the lyrics of an Avicii song seemed to make it all clear, "All this time I was finding myself, and I didn't know I was lost."

Whether I realized I was lost or not, ever since I figured out that having children was not a guaranteed future for us, I became a little obsessed with re-shaping my life and my purpose. Ok, a lot obsessed. Like that song continued, so did I, "Feeling my way through the darkness, guided by a beating heart, I can't tell where the journey will end, but I know where to start." For the first time in my life I was vision-less, but I was an eternal optimist, or hope-timist as I called it, and so while I was lost, all hope was not. Guided by my heart, I put feelers out into the dark, hoping to find a new passion.

I had never had a 'plan B', yet I'd always had a lot of ideas. I was a schemer like my father. For some reason though, I felt I needed to start by implementing every idea I ever had, so strong was the urge to fill this empty void I'd been left with. I was determined not to say 'no' until I first had tried 'yes'. I approached this no differently than I did everything I did, with a lot of formulating and exploring. I took self-discovery courses, read self-help books, tapped into old passions and searched for new ones.

I created one list after another of things I felt I needed or wanted to accomplish with this different future. I made a list of my attributes, skills, and characteristics that I already knew I had but now had the time to focus on and cultivate. I even made a colour coded chart in Excel! Excel and colours were two of my strengths, you see.

47

Apparently I also needed to act on it. All of it. At that very moment. Maybe so I wouldn't have time to feel that ever expanding void. Maybe because I never was good at being idle. Being a natural born planner and scheduler, I planned and scheduled all these new goals of mine into my life, with next to no wiggle room. I even put nearly every one of them in my Outlook calendar, reminders and all. But I didn't account for 'life happens.'

And it did.

Of course it did.

What did I think I would do when work got crazy? How did I not see I had far too many priorities? Why didn't I slow down when the things I valued most began to suffer? My calendar reminders didn't stop appearing when those started. I was eventually hit by an anxiety attack, one of my worst, but amidst it all I continued to feel obligated to keep up with my schedule. After all, I had this person I was trying to become, it was my choice to make these priorities, these goals. I would guiltily press 'snooze' on all those reminders with good intentions of getting back to them all later, but they kept piling up. Of course, overwhelming me even more. I forgot to schedule time to simply just be. I realize now, in hindsight of course, that embracing the gifts God gave me didn't mean I had to use them all, and so frequently, and so immediately.

~ 11 ~

I didn't realize it at the time, but God was even using my mistakes during this searching. I was misguided but He was guiding. One of those things I blindly added to my plate ended up being just the step in the right direction that I needed. Of course, He had laid out some really irresistible bait for me. My church had recently begun hosting the Network program to understand our spiritual gifts, so that we could find our sweet spot for serving in a ministry. And this was perfectly aligned with the quest I was already on. As it turns out, my Myers-Briggs personality type says we, "love understanding the nature of ourselves and others". This was a God nudge if I ever saw one! I mean, right as I was taking an inventory of my identity, interests and abilities, here was a course that was going to show me the giftings God had designed in me for my purpose. This course ended up giving me two key focuses that God really used to guide me down my path of discovery.

As if I wasn't already fascinated with the idea of profiling myself, learning about my spiritual giftings really clarified for me the difference between the skills I had acquired through experience versus the natural aptitudes I had. Having believed for so long that I was average at everything I did, when my gifts paralleled perfectly with my personality profiles, both Myers Briggs and

Enneagram, I was astounded at the long list of things I excelled at! I felt like I was truly getting to know myself for the first time in my life, yet I was not surprised about anything I discovered. This was the me I knew, but now I was growing to actually understand myself.

The second focus came when I was placed in a ministry at church that was a step towards my sweet spot. At the end of the course came a one-on-one session with someone who could offer discernment to help narrow down the options. My mentor suggested mentoring. It was not an entirely foreign concept but the moment he said it, it was like a light bulb had gone off! I felt something in my soul click! Like the next correct number in a combination lock had just been reached, the mechanism engages and releases the opening to the next level. I had no idea how many more chambers I had to get through to unlock my potential, but this was definitely one step closer.

After that interview I had another with a ministry leader, she led a group working on recovering from poor coping mechanisms in life, using a book called Changes That Heal. I barely knew this woman but I found myself opening up about the codependence and anxiety I had lived with all my life. How they had significantly interfered in my relationships. I shared how I had been gradually working through them over the years, and that my struggle with each of them seemed to be mostly over these days. She thought my past experiences made me an ideal facilitator, but more so I was excited I had my next opportunity to address some hang-ups I still hadn't fully dealt with. She gave me the book and study material for the group program, which began in a few months, to see if I was interested. She invited me to come see her once I read it, and I could decide then if I would be a mentor/facilitator for one of the table groups.

I was a self-development book addict so I soaked it up quickly, and the truths I learned not only shed light on the why of my problems, but the how of overcoming them as well. It was transformative! Not only did it give me perspective on my past but it gave me a whole new view of my future. And if I was one day blessed to have children, I knew this would be my go to book in raising them.

From my research into my personality, I already knew I was a helper. I wanted to walk with people and support people in transformation, growing beyond our hurts into wholeness. I already knew I wanted to help people who were struggling with the codependence and anxiety I was once crippled by, but once I read this book, I actually *knew* I could help them. I returned to the ministry leader with an eager yes, and within a month I was leading a group of people through their own personal transformations. Within a year, I was a leader in that expanded ministry, where I led a support group for women dealing specifically with codependence, anxiety, depression, eating addiction and other various hang-ups. Being there to support these women, whether in a group or one-on-one, showed me exactly where my strengths were. It also eventually led to my desire to return to school a few years later, to become a counselor. I finally knew what I wanted to be 'when I grew up'!

But even more than the gift of seeing more and more of my core self, the self I knew but hadn't really understood or appreciated, I was receiving another gift. I received the gift of seeing more and more of God, the God I knew but hadn't really understood or appreciated.

Chapter five

"We don't know what we don't know." ~ Donald Rumsfeld

~ ~ ~

There is nothing quite like coming out of a season, or lifetime, of obliviousness. It really is hard to fathom a completely different reality until you are exposed to it. And when you fully encounter it, you can't imagine how you ever lived without this knowledge! This describes very well my relationship with God during my pregnant pause. My first taste of real doubt, and then my first taste of deep faith.

I grew up in a conservative Christian home where we talked about having relationship over religion, yet my relationship with God was severely lacking. I had always believed I was a very faith-filled person, I had been through very hard seasons before, during which I sometimes labelled myself victim, and sometimes survivor, and yet through it all my faith remained fairly status quo. I had brief moments of questioning but never doubt. But this label, infertile, it was lasting much longer than those previous labels. Those scars had been from pain scattered throughout the years, but this pain was deep and almost daily for years on end.

It took me quite a long time to realize that what I was experiencing was grief. Not just grieving the miscarriages, but mourning my lost dreams, my lost identity, my lost sense of normalcy, and much more. Every month. The stages of grief include anger, and during infertility grief, that is an exceptionally easy stage, especially with our unexplained infertility. Searching for answers where there were none. Searching for something to blame where no blame was found. Hope fading with every closed door, along with all sense of control. Then, suddenly you realize, God has all control, and instantly there is a place to lay the blame again.

This wasn't an immediate conclusion for me, but that resentment was something that seeped in through the cracks of my heart, which were widened with every heartbreak, until I felt my heart was on the verge of complete darkness. The day I waved the white flag on trying to conceive was the day I began my awakening to how black my heart had become. I did not trust God.

Over the next several years I would struggle with this trust on and off, over and over. It was a strange type of struggle because my faith in God still had a certain amount of status quo. I didn't doubt that God was good, I only doubted He planned for my life to be good. I didn't doubt God could do miracles, I just doubted He would bless me with one. I didn't doubt God loved me, I simply doubted God liked me. My understanding of His love diminished my ability to receive it. It also deceived me into believing that because I wasn't getting what I wanted, God's promises didn't apply to me. Thankfully, God doesn't stop loving or providing just because I can't believe He does.

~ | | ~

All of us want the big miracle. Something as obvious as those of Biblical proportions; the parting of the red sea, stopping the sun, raising the dead, walking on water. When people talked to me about hoping for my own miracle I was dreaming of the Mary scenario, an Immaculate Conception, and hoping against the Sarah & Abraham situation of getting pregnant in my 90's. But there is a statement that has come to me over and over again in the last ten years or so that I couldn't forget. God much prefers to work through His people than through the supernatural. He wants us to be involved in His family business, healing our illnesses and issues through the touch of our loved ones rather than being touched by an angel. I can say with certainty, this is how God was doing a healing work in me.

It started with my diving into ministry, still seeking out my meaning in life, and before long I met several women who would change my life. For the last eight years these women have mourned with me, believed for me, cried with me, beat down God's door for me. They are my prayer warriors and my cheerleaders. The beautiful thing about it was we were all walking through various struggles, and I was able to give just as much as I received. Having female friends like this was certainly not something I was used to. God kind of blew me away with such generous provision of deep and loving friendship. He clearly knew I needed it more than I ever had before.

While I'd had Christian friends before, there was a depth in these women I'd never encountered before. And it paralleled my own earnest desire to truly experience communion, with God and a community of believers. It was one thing to have things in common, to share certain life experiences or personality traits, values and interests, but for the first time I was connecting on a spiritual level, not just emotional. Only two years ago I learned that one of the ways I connect to God the best is relationally, my sacred pathway to relating to God. It showed me that spiritual growth comes most natural to me if I am experiencing God with other people, and through the experiences and words of others. It was no wonder the deeper my relationship with these women grew, the closer I felt to God.

It helped that several of these women had learned about God through different communities and denominations than I grew up in. The experiences they had relating to God were brand new to me and opened a whole new world of connecting to God. At first I was envious when they said they frequently heard from God. I wanted their seemingly effortless bond, not realizing all that had gone in to developing that. Yet, I was so hungry for it that I soaked in all they had to say about the ways they encountered God, and went about trying it for myself. And it worked! I was intensely hoping it would but was still so shocked when it actually did! The idea of being able to simply ask God a question, then waiting expectantly for an answer, and then actually *receiving* one was mind blowing to me! God certainly proved He was just as interested in talking to me as I was in talking to Him!

~ | | ~

Of course, like most relationships that are being taken to the next level, there were still some growing pains. Learning to communicate on a deeper level always has challenges, like understanding their lingo, asking the right questions and of course, interpretation. Sometimes I heard right, sometimes I heard wrong. At first it was devastating to have heard incorrectly. Sometimes I just wanted to go back to the ignorance of not knowing what it was like to hear God's voice. It somehow felt like a rejection. However, with the truths spoken through my friends, I realized I had a lot to learn, and a lot could get 'lost in translation' between mere human and God. Not to mention, there was a very active creep who was doing everything possible to throw static on my line to God. One of the women leading a church Bible study during this time refused to give the name of satan power, and I began to adopt her name for him, 'the creep'. Over the years I also learned to implement the insight she shared on fighting his interference.

I was now spurred on, and I began a mission to learn all I could about fostering this fellowship with God. Again, my researching default kicked in, I began reading books, talking to people, watching videos, and praying frequently. The more I heard from Him, the hungrier I was for more! It was in these conversations a whole new side to God was revealed to me, and as I understood Him better I also understood more about how I was created and why. It is a unique vantage point when you can discover how entirely significant you are to the Creator of everything, at the same time realizing He loves everyone this much. And therefore, He is working for all our good throughout His plans. He had shared with me all the ways He made me distinctly qualified for a very specific purpose, yet I was just one note in His symphonic masterpiece. The plans and ambitions I once had lost their grip on me, and soon they were no longer completely tied up with my purpose or identity, all I wanted was to find harmony in His beautiful composition.

~ | | ~

I still didn't know what a miracle in my life would entail, but I began believing God had some in store for me. Maybe I'd receive the miracle of a tremendously fulfilling purpose without children. Maybe I'd receive the miracle of getting pregnant after all. Maybe I'd receive the miracle of falling in love with someone else's children who needed my parental love. Or something else altogether, something else in the wide expanse of possibilities my God could provide! I no longer had such a narrow mind about what a miracle might be. God is capable of infinitely more than I can ever hope or imagine. I had dreamed of motherhood because in my limited understanding of myself, and the options that fulfilled me, that was all my imagination could conjure up. I finally understood there was no limit to what God could bless us with, something that could replace my dream with one that was even more meaningful to me. And that in itself was a miracle!

I believe that's the kind of miracle God wants me to expect. The kind that takes Him out of the short-sighted and ignorant box I put Him in. I used to put Him in a box that meant He agreed with my ideas of right and wrong. That meant He agreed that my judgement of fair was the correct one. Then He showed me how enormous the world is, and how He loves everyone equally, working for the good of all, not just me. I used to put Him in a box that said I deserved to be a mother because I was good, and He was bad if He didn't provide a child for me. Then He showed me how entitled that was, and that I don't deserve anything from Him at all. I used to put Him in a box where He couldn't possibly love parents who neglected or rejected their children. Then I met a woman who met God during her experience through an abortion. His ways are so immensely different from our ways.

There are still days that I hate that some of my perceptions of 'right' are not God's, but I don't think God expects me to understand, or even approve, of His plans. As I once heard Michelle Obama say in response to a question about responding to people who disagree with their position, "That's not what the people need us to be, is personally offended by criticism. They need someone who gets the job done." And how much more so does God choose to ignore our criticism of His authority and just go on loving us, every day. He silently, behind the scenes, gets the work done. He knows we don't see the whole picture, that we don't have the benefit of His omniscience, omnipotence and perfection. And it was only because I opened the door to having a real relationship with Him, having honest conversations with Him, that I grew to know without a shadow of a doubt that He not only loved me but truly liked me as well.

~ | | ~

In the two years after my conception hiatus, I finally came to a place where I treasured the relationship I formed with God more than I treasured being a mother. As much as I am ashamed to admit it, for a time children were my treasure above God, above my husband. But no man can serve two masters, for all the love and devotion I placed on having children, it spawned contempt for all the moments God or my husband asked for something opposing. What an awful thing to say, but it is true. Infertility is the best thing that could have happened for my faith, and therefore my marriage.

With prayer and petition comes His peace that passes understanding. This verse about peace, Philippians 4:6, became a mantra for me, first in unrelated anxiety, but then in the anxiousness of a dying dream. And God has been faithful in keeping this promise for me, the more I petition Him in prayer the more peace I have that passes my understanding. And not only is it the kind of peace that is "an irrational sense of emotional calm", it really does surpass understanding. I found I no longer had the need to understand why. It's not that ignorance is bliss, because for me it still isn't, but when God chooses not to reveal the answers to me that I seek, then I simply rest in my trust in my God. It is I who is in a box, with limits on my understanding and reach and power, not God.

Choosing to trust will not be without its challenges. Choosing His plan over mine and choosing to be aligned with His purposes will be a test of my limitations. Infertility has been one of the hardest things I've ever walked through, but it would have been so much harder if I had stayed 'living by sight' rather than 'living by faith'. I don't expect moving forward will be much easier. What I do expect is that He will continue to give me that transcending peace in choosing Him. Living by faith allowed me to be me because it allowed God to be God. Trusting God allowed Him to work in and through me, allowing me to live my best life.

Yet. At the same time, after all that, I didn't feel like He had asked me to forfeit my own dreams completely. In one of those God conversations, when I was brave enough to ask once again what my future as a mother might look like, I heard, "Talk to your husband." I was actually quite anxious about bringing up the subject with him again, after all, I declared with great conviction I was done with trying to try. On top of that, he had given no indication his heart had changed, as far as I knew, he was still as reluctant as ever.

Our ninth wedding anniversary was just around the corner and I had planned a weekend away an hour outside the city, so I decided I was going to broach the subject with him once again on that ride home. After, so it wouldn't ruin the weekend together, you know? I was that nervous. However, I was also really hopeful, and I wanted to test out my hearing. Did I hear God correctly? I would know the second I got his response.

Chapter **six**

"No way over it, no way around it, if we want it we have to go
through it. Fight for love.....love will always win."
~ Garth Brooks "Love Will Always Win"

~ ~ ~

We are not a couple who fights. Even what we would
consider a fight has been very quiet compared to some
quarrels I've witnessed. Just recently I heard about an
animal comparison to marital fighting styles, and at this
time in our lives we were both turtles - sucking ourselves
back into our shell to escape the conflict. When things
got tough, we got silent. When I hit pause it got very
silent.

Even after we thought we'd learned our lesson about not
communicating enough (preceding our biggest 'fight'
ever, all 30 seconds of it). Somehow we were still
keeping some of our feelings to ourselves, keeping secrets
from each other. On top of not fully sharing my doubts
about my identity and about God, I had a bigger secret

worry. My biggest secret worry was that I had hurried into a marriage without God's blessing, and now I was being punished by being with someone who didn't want children as much as I did. I wasn't as close to God when we met, or even when we married, I wasn't asking Him for guidance, wasn't listening for direction.

Yet, I refused to let my mind go too far down that road. Whenever it cropped up I would remind myself that I had too much evidence to contradict that. Until this struggle, there was nothing that could have convinced me we weren't created for each other. And so I latched on to the opposite end of that thought spectrum. Having a child was supposed to be about strengthening our togetherness, but all the trying was doing was dividing us. So I was choosing us over a baby.

~ | | ~

I thought somehow that, even though it would be difficult for me to give up, it would lighten the burden on both of us. That instantly the obstacle separating us would simply disappear. That was not the case, in fact the opposite was true, though it took me a long time to realize the increased distance was actually related. My husband gradually grew more distant physically and emotionally, and seemed to grow more irate and aggravated than before. I was playing a guessing game with him for months trying to understand whatever it was that went wrong.

It was getting worse and worse, and we got quieter and quieter, until his negativity actually triggered an anxiety attack. Like I said, we took our conflicts into our internal worlds, and there I examined, processed, digested it all. I could not figure out what was going on. I had a history of generalized anxiety and I had become more aware that these inner dialogues about conflict, if left unresolved for too long, created a cavity of uncomfortable pressure in my chest that would grow until the conflict ended. I sensed that inflation of worry expand, which only increased my anxious thoughts, and within a week it was like it had taken over my torso. I had trouble breathing, it felt like a 20 lb weight was sitting on top of my chest. I tried to go to work anyway, because who takes time off for emotional issues that they are not even courageous enough to deal with. Fortunately there was the mixed blessing of working with a friend who also suffered from anxiety, and I went to her for support. Without telling her too much, she encouraged me to take some sick time and deal with the root cause.

So I did. The conclusion I came to was that I had to get him to confront the downward spiral we were in. Even if he only faced it for me, to stop the anxiety attack that just would not lift until this was fixed. Finally, being forced to think about it and answer for it, he realized it had to do with not being able to have a baby. That is the last thing I would have thought was troubling him! He surprised me by confessing a lot of the pain, disappointment, and frustration in his life was due in large part to the pain of not being able to 'give' me my biggest passion and purpose, motherhood. That it was his fault. Somehow in that confession, finally sharing that pain unlike we had before, something changed. The impact of that shift wasn't immediate of course. But. It was like we had the same epiphany, and we both started turning to God with our pain instead of internalizing it. And the more God moved in our circumstances, the more we wanted to share the victories with each other.

~ | | ~

There is a common marriage principle taught among Christians, that the closer each spouse is to God, the closer they draw to each other. Whoever is teaching this out will demonstrate by drawing an equilateral triangle, with God at the top and each spouse being the other two points. If only one person draws closer to God, the distance between the couple remains the same but if they both grow closer to God, they grow closer to each other as well. This was taught at a marriage seminar we attended in the first few months of marriage, but at that time we were both equally connected to God, and so of course it made sense. Over the years though we had both changed our height, and direction, on that triangle several times, yet weren't able to figure out why we felt a distance between us. Looking back now, if I believed in regret, I would have been more serious about pursuing marriage counselling. That one marriage seminar and a few books was not enough to help us through that rough terrain. I sometimes wonder how much quicker we would have resolved things if...but I have tried to vow off 'what ifs'. So, eight years later, our connection to God was finally shortening the distance between us. Even if we didn't realize it in the moment, we were living that triangle principle out.

The combination of seeking out God's peace, and our own purposes within His designs, led us both to an increasing desire to be involved in more ministries at Church. At first we had different interests, different paths, but then a new ministry was brought into our Church and we both ended up serving there. It meant a commitment of every Friday, starting right after dinner until ten pm, every week of the year. It stretched us both right out of our comfort zones! Yet it also gave us very important tools for addressing the various hurts we'd accumulated our whole lives. It also showed us incredible insight into how God was using our hurts to support others who were hurting as well. And it didn't only help those we served but it helped us help each other too.

The bonus of doing ministry together was the opportunity to take a meandering drive afterward. It was a chance to debrief from the night, but then also a chance to share our hearts in ways we weren't used to doing as frequently. But there we were, every Friday night, making the most of this organic opportunity to be vulnerable with each other. Not only did we connect on a level of shared purpose like never before, we exposed a depth of our hearts which we had never let see the light of day, never mind allowing anyone else to see. Being given the materials and the moments to process such healing truths, and with each other, was such an incredibly powerful agent of change in our individual and united lives.

~ | | ~

The second year of our procreation vacation, I am sure we broke our dating records with how much we showered each other in love. I received flowers three times that year, more than I had in our entire marriage before that. Even better, he hand washed the dishes twice when the dishwasher broke down! Be still my heart.

It was also serendipitous that we met an amazing couple through one of the ministry involvements at Church, who became our mentors. They were not only incredible as individuals but they were one of the most loving couples we had ever met. And they were married as many years as I had been alive! They demonstrated, and encouraged, a lot of affection for each other, it was almost impossible not to be positively influenced by them.

Between our increased vulnerability and affection, I believe a compassion for each other's pain was discovered. One we didn't know we were lacking, but now was a strong empathetic force that made it so much easier to love and support one another. Of course, being completely open and honest about our hang-ups and heartbreaks was a huge component. How can you feel for, and with, someone if you don't even know what they are feeling? It also didn't hurt that we also grew to trust God more, which made it easier to let go of those hurts. We didn't get as caught up in the hardships life was still throwing our way and we both had peace about life not happening according to our will.

What a remarkable effect it can have on a relationship when we can let go of our worries, ok, most of our worries to God. Amazing things happen when that fear, doubt, and unease is no longer creating discord, when it no longer has the power to divide. What God has united, let no one separate.

~ | | ~

So, rewinding back to that day. That day I was going to reintroduce the biggest hindrance to our 'happily ever after'. After our year long love-fest, why was I still nervous about bringing up the subject of returning to the world of baby-making? Largely it was because I didn't want to ruin the magical mojo we now had by bringing that enormous stress source back to the marriage bed.

Our ninth anniversary celebration weekend had gone even better than I could have anticipated! It was a very sweet time together, so when we got in the car to head home, I once again questioned shortening the bliss with that topic.   Even despite having brought up many uncomfortable topics during car rides over the last year, this one gave me pause. But then I got that Holy Spirit nudge, and a little dash of courage, then went for it. I shared that God had changed my heart towards the idea of trying again, and that I had asked Him how I would know if it was ok to start down that path again. I told hubby that my answer had been I was supposed to talk to him about it. Then, I held my breath.

Then, I received another miracle! He said he too had experienced God changing his heart! Over the last few months he had found himself suddenly having his own deep desire for children! I was so shocked, I had not expected that much enthusiasm or longing to pour from him in regards to being able to have his own children. He was 31 now, maybe his biological clock finally kicked in? Whatever the reason God shifted his heart, I was so grateful we could start again, and this time, we'd start on the same page.

Chapter seven

"You gain strength, courage, and confidence by every experience in which you really stop to look fear in the face. You are able to say to yourself, 'I lived through this horror. I can take the next thing that comes along'." ~ Eleanor Roosevelt

~ ~ ~

I had let fear shape most of my life. Even my initial dream of motherhood and what I wanted it to look like, started off as fears. I had let those fears put my dream in a box, just like I had put God in one. Then came the day I decided that dream was dead, but I had never actually peered into the box to see for sure. I thought it was easier to deal with if I believed it was dead. As it turns out, it was more like Schrödinger's cat. For those of you who aren't scientists or avid fans of The Big Bang Theory, Schrödinger's cat is a physics experiment that essentially states that until you open that box and know for sure, that cat exists in both states, dead and alive. Those two years I did a lot of examining but had never opened that box, until one day I prayed about it and decided it was time to peek inside. Wouldn't you know, my dream leaped out alive and kicking!

One of the books we both read during that season, The Me I Want to Be, talked about God's purposes for us and how when He creates something strong in us, He doesn't simply decide to scrap it. He made us that way for a reason, and just like he doesn't change an oak seed to grow a rose or vice versa, He doesn't change His original design in us. However, our perception of what it means to be an oak might be different than God's. After all some oaks stand in a forest for their entire lives, planting seeds, giving shade, but others are created into beautiful furniture, like desks, wardrobes, cradles. And we were certain this was a God-given dream of ours, to have a family together. So we moved forward down that road again, trusting God would lead the way to however this dream would manifest.

Not many months later I was practicing my conversations with God, trying once again to ask questions about the future of our parentage. After several occasions of hearing correctly I was hopeful I would get an answer that was a little more concrete, but wasn't holding my breath either. I will just as often get pictures as I get words that pop into my mind when I am in listening prayer, but this time I saw the letter "J". Since it was the month of June I immediately asked if it was this month, or better yet, the next month, July, my birthday month. To that I heard the word January, and clearly sensing my reluctance to accept I heard accurately, God then gave me a picture of a calendar with January in bold type-face across the top. I don't know exactly what I expected but that level of clarity had not even been on my radar!

~ | | ~

The next six months ended up being quite the rollercoaster in all walks of life. My third nephew was born a few weeks late a few weeks later, an adorable addition to my collection of kiddos, my heart ever expanding with each one. Then a few weeks after that my mom suffered suddenly from a heart attack. Thankfully it happened in a hospital and she survived it as well as the triple bi-pass surgery one day later. It was a shock because it was actually my dad we had been worried about, experiencing chest pains and fainting spells. The worries I had previously, about my parents not being around to meet my children resurfaced. I anxiously awaited those two days for my mom to regain consciousness to tell her we were trying again, and that I had prayed for her to survive so she could meet my baby one day. But that wasn't the end of family health problems or loss, four other major health problems arose in our immediate and extended family during that time.

And in between the falls there was also the soaring. We had finally found a small community of believers that came to be like family to us, not just for a season but a few still are to this day. Including my best friend, and my first true kindred spirit in every way. Then, after ten rollercoaster years at his job, the hubby found a new calling and went back to school. We were both thrilled to see a passion and joy return to him as he explored all that this new path could mean for him, and for us. Starting school again after ten years, and while still working full time, was certainly going to be a challenge, but one he was eager for.

It was a hard yet happy six months, however by the time December's time of the month came I had almost forgotten the promise. Yeah right. Ok, I had convinced myself to not think about it on a daily basis, and it had moved to the backburner in my mind. I was a little disappointed I wasn't pregnant on time to make Christmas present announcements, but I was optimistic, there was still next month!

~ | | ~

The real doubts started a day or two before I would have known. My ovulation date was usually cycle day 15 or 16 and I was about day 22 when I was pouring my worry out at God's feet. It had been several years since I wondered if I was pregnant, but my heart had muscle memory. It knew we had been here before, and suddenly all those feelings of loss were just as fresh and raw again. My thoughts raced. I wasn't about to test, not until day 44, I had vowed this time. So, instead I asked God for a sign.

I asked for a specific sign. I have a huge love of rainbows, for all their colours and promises, which prompted me to ask for a rainbow. In the middle of January, in Winnipeg, also affectionately known as Winterpeg. I even laughed at myself, the audaciousness! "Now there's a challenge for you God! I guess You'll have to give me a sundog!" No rainbow appeared that day. Or the next week. However at less than one week late, as I forgot something my husband had asked for, he slyly suggested, "Baby brain?" And with that, I knew he knew too. I wondered if God had refused my test but gave me a sign through my very intuitive husband.

Suddenly I forgot all my doubts, this was going to be the first time we were pregnant and both knew and both were ecstatic! After our history we were still cautious, not testing until two weeks late, not telling anyone until we tested, not telling most until three months along. But between the two of us we were having a merry old time celebrating. We were renewing our vows for our tenth anniversary in six weeks and had all sorts of reveal plans in mind. We calculated when the little one would be born and it would be so close to their daddy's birthday. We were thrilled we'd get to share this experience with our dear friends who had announced their own pregnancy only one month before. We planned out what the baby dedication would be like, with all the dozens of people who had prayed alongside us for that day. All those things most couples get to do the first time they find out their pregnant, we finally got to share those moments, and it was so sweet. This rollercoaster ride took us to a pinnacle we had never reached together before. Maybe it was the 'high altitude' but we were euphoric.

That is until unexpectedly the ride dive bombed into a spiral downward. It happened at work on day 42, the count of days old ended at 26, two days shy of two weeks late. I could barely manage the words to tell him as I picked him up after work, the ride home was a blur, figuratively and literally. I probably shouldn't have been driving. Gravity had no mercy on us, and as we sunk into the pit, I had that familiar sickening disassociation of leaving my heart and stomach to free fall behind me.

I don't remember a whole lot of that evening except that he had to go to church that night for one of the ministries he served in, and he was standing near the entrance, torn about leaving me for his commitments. Once again, this was a first, mourning the loss together. This time I could not hide the despair from him, and I knew I didn't have to. Everything I felt, he felt too, which made it easier and harder all at once. Finally I felt that mourning a life so brief was normal, but at the same time I had to watch the heart break of the one I loved most. We were crying and embracing, and it was the most beautiful intersection of pain and love I'd ever known. That valley we had dropped into felt more like a void, but at least we anchored each other. Finally, I told him it was ok to go, then in true 'us' fashion, he said something funny that burst the tension when I burst out laughing. We were going to be ok. Not today, but someday.

~ | | ~

The next few weeks and months were full of firsts we had never experienced after a miscarriage before. First and foremost we decided to be honest and let all our close friends and family know about our loss. We simply didn't have the energy to hide our heartache, and we knew we were in healthy relationships that we could trust with our pain. Friends from age 17 to 60+ were instrumental in letting us authentically process our grief, and supporting us in such a deeply healing way. I'm certain they were God's hands, pulling us up out of that valley when we didn't have the strength to face that uphill battle on our own.

Then there was the first realization I was prone to depression during loss. I had begun doubting myself, listening to the lie that somehow I deserved this. Also the doubting that I had even heard God correctly, feeling unworthy of being able to hear Him. The anxiety of those burdens weighed on me until I had another panic attack and then the depression moved in. It was not quite able to fully grab a hold of me, but certainly casting a shadow that was hard to evade. Most people said the depression would dissipate when the grief did, but it didn't. This led to awareness that I had faced this before in my other miscarriages, and through other very difficult situations in my past, uncovering a deeper disorder than the grief alone could account for.

This wasn't the only health discovery that was made as a result of my miscarriage. For the first time in my life, information about the reproductive system was shared with me that gave me new insights into what the cause might be. Or at the very least, what might be some obstacles we could remove. Despite the fertility clinic not providing this information to me five years earlier, I was still motivated to go back to my doctor and talk about my miscarriages. Once again this led us to pursue a specialist who could possibly provide some new options.

I was quite often surprised, and still am, at the amount of strength we had to face all the fallout from this failure. And it was amazing all the good that was already coming from such an unbearable situation. One we'd never wish for, obviously, but, in hindsight, would also not undo.

~ l l ~

Unfortunately, there was one area it took more time for the good to show itself. Even though we saw the hand of God working through our hurt, I couldn't help but shift from self-doubt to doubting God again. I knew I heard Him correctly, He told me I was going to be pregnant in January, and I was! Until He took it back! When that doubt was first creeping in near the end, I had begged Him not to let it happen. And for the next few days I couldn't say anything else to Him because I didn't know what else to say. What else was there to ask for but life? And when that prayer didn't get answered the way I wanted, the distance between us was instant. I continued to have nothing to say to Him.

I felt Him trying to reach out to comfort me but just couldn't accept it. He pursued me with music, and visions, as well as words and gifts through friends, determined to show me He was grieving with me. I could feel Him persisting, all He wanted to do was love on me so He could heal my hurts. The last vision that finally moved my heart back towards Him was a picture of me in the dark pit I knew I was in. Then. The picture started zooming out, and I could begin to see some formations of the pit, some creases started showing. It was growing gradually brighter until I finally saw myself in the crook of His elbow as He cradled me.

After that, it still wasn't easy talking to God, but I gradually began to pick up where I left off. Other than the listening part, I expressly tried to turn off my ability to listen. I just couldn't bear to hear anything that could be a spark of hope near the open wound of my heart. I was pretty sure grief was flammable. Instead I turned to music as my salve, one way I felt I could safely let God's love and truth wash over me, bringing me comfort.

The other gift I had was the friends God spoke so clearly through. They had not changed, they were still the amazing God girls who had been my guiding light to His presence once before. They continued to shine that light for me to follow once again. And there were more of them now then there were three years prior, like a team of magnets whose pull only got stronger the more there were. Before long I was plunging back into our deep dives, into God's presence, eager to soak it up once again. I thought I had received a revelation of who God was before, but He began showing me even greater depths of Himself, and myself, that worked to once again solidify my faith. I was never going to doubt Him again.

After the first half of that year, I would have said I had finally come to a point where I could handle any dark days. I had made it back up from the bottom of the pit and I was stronger for it. My faith was stronger for it. My marriage was stronger for it. And while that miscarriage was the hardest, in a strange way it was also the easiest.

Yet. The next 16 months brought with it a whole new series of struggles, ones that would test my declaration to never doubt again.

~ | | ~

We were no strangers to loss by now. The loss of death. The losses of infertility. The loss of faith. The loss of purpose and identity. At the same time we learned to be grateful for what we did have, not merely accepting it as consolation prizes, but truly appreciating how blessed they made us.

We had a stronger, wider, healthier circle of loved ones than ever before. We had well-paying jobs that could be challenging, but we worked with people who had become friends. They also afforded us free evenings to dedicate to each other and our community. We had reached a level of faith that gave us a peace and freedom like we'd never known. We both had new insights into our purpose and future careers that we were passionate about. A new dream we could share was developing as we were planning to take counselling classes alongside each other soon. I had also finally begun to find healing from lifelong body-image issues, through the recovery group we belonged to, and the love and encouragement of my girlfriends. These were not small things in our lives.

Can you guess what happened next? It seemed like in the blink of an eye, it all started to unravel once again. It began with our communities. All of them. Some of our most significant mentors moved away, and one passed away. The recovery group we volunteered with was going through a six month transformation period and it was harder to find support from our peers during that stressful time. Then our biggest support, our small church group of 'friends like family', whom we did life with on an almost daily basis, was slowly going their own separate ways. Including my best friend who was moving half way around the world to become a missionary, for who knew how long.

Then there was our jobs, both steadily getting more and more stressful for various reasons. We were to the point where we were praying daily for God to free us from the environments that were becoming increasingly toxic, that even large salaries did not make it worth dealing with. We were both still at the early stages for schooling and a new career for either of us in that field was a long way off.

And to top it all off my body went through hormonal hell with a new treatment we thought could help our final diagnosis of poor egg viability. We had dove back into the doctor's waiting room, but once again what started out as hopeful ended up being just more pain. Emotionally, and without a doubt, physically. My weight skyrocketed and my self-worth plummeted, and all for zero results. I then switched to a more natural route which ended up improving my hormone levels and fertility as a whole, yet with no viable pregnancies. Despite the faith and trust we placed in God when we decided to try again, I could not fight off the depression. It seemed to get the best of me for far too long, only contributing more to my body issues with all the emotional eating.

We had overcome so much in the last few years, and it had given us the strength and courage to find our way through all that. Still it seemed the more we fought it off, the more our fears morphed and came back at us with a new angle and new determination. The new and hopeful developments in our life one-by-one joined the pause and we ended up still stuck in the waiting room, one that existed outside the doctor's office.

Chapter eight

"Follow every rainbow, till you find your dream."
~ The Sound of Music

~ ~ ~

In November 2014, many of my most recent prayers finally found some answers. I was laid off from my longest, and best paying, job up to that point. However, considering how the company had transitioned in the eighteen months prior, and how miserable I had become due to those changes, this was such a blessing. I had been pleading with God to release me from that job for nearly a year, and had even started school again to change careers only two months prior. I thought God's silence had been indifference but as it turned out, He was indeed listening to me and looking out for me all along. Including a handsome severance that took this blessing to the next level, and I began to view it as more like a sabbatical. It was a chance for much needed rest from the many various stresses I had been dealing with for the past few years. It ended up being over seven months off before I found a new job, and as I was able to explore all the freedom I was now afforded, I began to dream more freely about what brought me fulfillment and joy. I spent that free time working on what had previously got me through my difficult years of rest from reproduction, things I loved but that I had been certain my recent stress was keeping me from.

My first order of business, I was determined to return to connecting to God at a deeper level. While I hadn't fallen into doubt again through the last few years, it had been a season of strain as I strived to earn God's divine intervention in my life. With this recent miracle, now I was able to say I trusted Him implicitly, no matter what happened going forward, and I wanted to dive deep into His loving presence.

I also wanted to spend time focusing on family. More than ever family was so important to me, both our family of two, and my immediate family. I felt like I had been missing too much of the precious moments in my nieces and nephews lives. They were growing up so fast, and I wanted to have a more significant role in their lives. I also wanted to devote more to my husband, and how I could be a wife that blessed him in any season going forward. I knew this could be a season of rekindling the fire that had dwindled while we had little left for fuel.

And God knew my heart had been yearning for former deep connections, the space for them was vast and vacant for too long. The space He gave me not only made room for that, but also opened doors to develop new ones. I took every opportunity to put myself in the path of companionship, making my penchant for extroversion and fellowship a priority, as well as creating a space to seek accountability and encouragement as I figured out what was next for my life. I found new places of belonging that couldn't have been more perfect for my next season to come.

The first six weeks of unemployment were good for regrouping, restoring, and re-affirming my priorities that would shape not only the rest of my unemployment, but hopefully all future seasons, working or not. I found it a little funny and ironic when it came to December 31st and I had this all thought out and put down in a list, but I still insist they were not New Year's resolutions.

~ | | ~

This little list also led me to return to my love of art. Once I remembered how much life it gave me to create, I was reminded of the creative dreams I used to have as a child. During this time, another fear was exposed. My fear of failure, especially in the creative arts, which directed me to more practical careers where competition and comparison were less. I had convinced myself that the only way my artistic talent would have room in my life was once I was a mother. Then I could incorporate them into how I raised my children. God showed me how creativity was engrained in my purpose, it was not just for this reprieve, it was not simply a hobby, and it was not only with children one day.

I didn't realize it in that moment, it took another few years for that, but I learned that there is often a script in our heads that tells us there is only one path to accomplishing a certain dream of ours. We know that we are meant for that dream, but for some reason all the traditional means to that end do not seem possible or achievable. Often, a lie that gets planted by the creep is to blame. Yet, we are a species bent on purpose and fulfillment and meaning, so our minds will find a way.

Too often, we don't turn to the one who planted the dream. Instead, in a stretch of the imagination, our minds will create a scenario where suddenly we have the answer. We know a way that we are certain will make our dreams happen. Very often, I've noticed, the answer we conclude lies within our children. And often, without us even realizing it, our dreams become intertwined with having children, and all our fulfillment is now riding on that one thing, the ability to have a family. This was true for me, and that script I was trying to force into motherhood was actually being an artist.

There were so many revelations happening during this season, it was hard to keep up, or to understand how they all fit together. It was like viewing an incomplete puzzle, the outside edges were done but otherwise there were about half a dozen semi-complete little pictures within the big picture, and my mind was spinning trying to figure out how they all connected. How did they all fit together to make up my purpose?

~ | | ~

Right before I found my next job, my exploration took a new turn. There was now also the possibility my school was ending the Counselling program I had just started, only one fifth complete. At the same time, I was encouraged by Employment Insurance to attend career and job fairs, which is where I stumbled across a talk on Life Coaching. The next thing I knew I was researching it and signing up for the next certification course coming to Winnipeg. Of course, old fears came to haunt me, the self-doubt crept in while I waited for that course. I had almost talked myself out of it by that weekend. But, that was too much money to waste by skipping out, and so I told myself all the 'at least' statements I could in order to gather my courage to go.

I walked through the doors one early September Saturday to find the instructor playing some tunes as he prepared for the class that was still 25 minutes from starting. It took me a moment to figure out the song because, even though he was alone, he played his music softly. But once I did recognize the tune I was hit by a wave of certainty that I did indeed belong there. That and a wave of pure emotion, as I realized how long God had been preparing me for that moment. I still get all choked up every time I think of that feeling I got, as I stood in that classroom, when I understood just how much God is doing for us behind the scenes.

The song was 'A Sky Full of Stars' by Coldplay and God had been bombarding me with it for a full year. Then He used it to align with another song about counting stars instead of dollars, giving me hope there was a new job on the horizon. One where I could pursue my purpose rather than the paycheck, the one thing that kept me from quitting. He used it to spur on a tremendous conversation with a friend on a road trip. One that led to deep revelations about being His star, His diamond, reflecting His light. Then a month later He used it to comfort me in the midst of my best friend's wedding. A wedding that meant she was now living in a different country than me, hours and hours away. 'A Sky Full of Stars' actually reminded me of another song on her wedding day. One from an old Disney movie, that sings "and even though I know how very far apart we are, it helps to think we might be wishing on the same bright star."

For the next month after her wedding that song continued to play more and more frequently, no matter what station I flipped to. Shortly after my layoff, it slowed down a little, once in a while I'd hear it just when I needed a confirmation of where to place my hope. Like that morning, when I walked into a classroom, so unsure if it was where I belonged.

It was.

That course turned out to be so much more than I could have ever anticipated. Yes, the material was good. Yes, the instructor was good. But it was the intangibles that blew my mind that weekend. It was the fact our instructor was a former pastor, and he reconciled for me how to fit faith into secular work in this industry. It was the fact I felt very confident in the material and just knew this aligned perfectly with who I was. It was the fact that the women I was grouped with, who we were supposed to practice the tools with, spoke insight into my life that has changed how I see myself to this day. I didn't just leave that program a certified Life Coach, I left there seeing myself through God's eyes in a way I never had before.

My biggest take-away from that weekend was that nothing is insignificant. I could have seen that song playing over and over as irrelevant. I could have seen my Counselling program ending two courses in as inconvenient. I could have seen that glimpse into Life Coaching at that career fair as interesting but immaterial. I could have seen a 2 day certification program as too inferior. And even though I hadn't seen them that way, I really had no idea how significant they actually were until that day.

~ I I ~

After all that, my counselling courses ended up resuming after all. Throughout those remaining eight courses I continued to gain insights into my true purpose that still didn't deviate from my mother's heart. Half way through counselling courses I was in a Child & Youth Development class, and what I was learning in class triggered both my mom heart and my helper/counselling heart. It was then I realized I could use my passion & knowledge for more than being a mother. I also realized that my level of desire to do so was actually just as strong as my longing to be a mother. I had never had that before, where there was something else in life I wanted to do as much as I wanted to be a mother. As I worked to develop my counselling skills, I was increasingly being validated for my aptitude in it across various relationships. I saw it positively impact lives more and more, and I fully realized this meaningful work of nurturing healing was what I was meant to do.

As I looked back through this process of discovering myself I had yet another revelation. This natural capacity I had for walking alongside people during painful situations, and passion for helping them overcome. This earned ability for empathy and instinctive aptitude for actively listening. This had all been within me much longer than I ever realized. The winding road that felt like it had been detour after detour had actually been refining my compassion and character with experiences. But I had within me what I'd needed for this destination all along.

As if to make that point stick, one last surprise discovery happened through my counselling courses. A lot of our classes were designed to make us aware of the various specialties we could have as counselors. One class on theories explained how some theories worked very well with art therapy! I knew art therapy existed yet it had been a long forgotten piece of information that clearly needed exhuming. I just about jumped out of my seat with excitement when I read that! Not only that, but I should have made the connection on my own. I had been using various creative processes during my own struggles throughout the years to help me heal after all. I would express my varied heartaches through poetry over the years, and I would play with colours on canvas when my spirit needed uplifting. I knew art had helped me heal, yet the concept of art therapy had remained completely off my radar until that moment. I was flooded with ideas on how I could incorporate art therapy into my career and it gave me so much joy!

That was not the end of my discoveries in 2015 though, God was not finished yet. Apparently He was just as determined to make the most of my sabbatical, and undistracted time, as I was. In the early version of our transformed ministry a year prior, I had attempted to create a safe place for women to find support during infertility. Knowing how much I needed that myself during the hardest moments. I felt like I could finally put my experiences to use for the benefit of other hurting women. This was not a success but it was a seed.

In the Spring of 2015 I was invited to a women's retreat through one of the communities I had joined that year, where God showed me more insights for my path. Through Jesus' words in John 12:24, "Unless a kernel of wheat falls to the ground and dies, it remains only a single seed. But if it dies, it produces many seeds." And then a few chapters later He talks about staying connected to Him in order to be fruitful. I knew then God was showing me what He was doing through my infertility. Where one dream was dying, literally, so that many more could come to fruition. Not more than a few hours later I bumped into a woman I had met in my infertility support group. She had attended the group so she could actually find a place to give support, not receive it. Suddenly we were having a conversation about how we could still find a way to create a safe and supportive space for women suffering in silence with infertility, something we were determined to figure out. Then, to cap off the weekend, the leaders provided each woman in attendance a card with a word from God they had received as they prayed over each of us. Mine was fruitful. I knew then God had so much more in store for me in this budding dream of walking alongside women who were stuck in the same pregnant pause as I was.

It was by no means the last piece of the puzzle. There were still many gaps in the bigger picture, but for once I saw pieces connecting that I had previously thought were random and irrelevant to one another. Bridges were being built between my wide variety of capabilities and circumstances. I suddenly awakened to the truth, this had been my path all along, I had never really been lost!

Chapter nine

"Gratefulness is not what you feel after times of joyfulness. Gratefulness is what you have to choose to get to times of joyfulness." ~ Ann Voskamp

~ ~ ~

Between my new job, developing a life coaching business, finishing my counselling program, and still trying to maintain the essential priorities I established during my sabbatical, the next few years flew by. I was also working hard to incorporate the truths I was learning through my education and apply them to myself, keeping myself anchored yet hopeful and healthy. Mindfulness was something I was especially interested in incorporating into my daily life, working at my gratefulness to increase my joy as much as possible. There were still ups and downs that made this easier and/or harder, depending on the day. Overall though, gratitude and joy were becoming much more of a natural disposition for me.

This struck me in an exceptionally brilliant moment one day. It happened right before my last class of my second last semester. I was thoroughly enjoying the way the strong sun light and invading dark storm were wrestling over control of the sky. I happen to be a sky addict, enamoured with pretty much every natural phenomenon that happens in the sky. Rainbows, sunsets and sunrises, constellations and galaxy views, but also storms with enormous clouds and lightening. With this sunset and storm colliding, I couldn't take my eyes off the heavens. If I hadn't had a class, and my final grade presentation, I would have stood outside in the rain laced air all evening to enjoy it. I soaked it in until the very last minute and then as I entered the college I noticed how peaceful and relaxed I felt. This was of note because I normally get the pre-presentation jitters, but they were nowhere to be found.

Later at home, as I was unwinding with a quick scroll through Facebook, I saw someone's photo of a beautiful rainbow from that evening. And then another and another. Then I saw someone's magnificent photo of a giant double rainbow that stretched across the whole sky! "Really?" I thought. I had missed out on these remarkable rainbows! Yet, interestingly, I immediately realized something in that green-eyed moment. I have previously been caught up in moments when I feel I am missing out on my idea of ideal, focusing on the unfairness that someone else got it when I didn't. When it means so much to me. That fear of missing out almost caused me to diminish the gorgeous sky I did have the opportunity to enjoy! Metaphorically, we are told to tolerate the storm because a rainbow will follow, and I did much more than tolerate. I relished in it, with no expectation of seeing a rainbow after. The sky I witnessed was inspiring and gave me a few moments of healing, no less than a rainbow would have accomplished.

It was in that moment of awareness I wondered how many spectacular moments had I diminished over the years because I wasn't getting my dream. Because I wasn't getting my dream of the ideal family experience. Or anything else in life I was more concerned with the ideal than the actual. My desire to be mindful stemmed from wanting to recognize God's love and generosity in my life. If I had learned anything through my journey this far, it was that those moments won't always look like a typical blessing. But! That doesn't lessen the healing and joy I can receive from them, if I will only recognize them for what they are.

~ | | ~

This mindfulness was also helping me examine my feelings as the circle of life, aging and death, became more and more of a reality with every year that passed. One day I had lunch with my dad and even while he saw the decline in independence with the increasing age of his friends and family, he was still very resistant to the idea his age changes his abilities. He still thought "I'm young enough". One could argue in some aspects he was, he was playing volleyball with family just a little while ago, at the age of seventy-one! And with those who were mostly half his age or younger! Then, in other ways my sisters and I noticed aging we had never been aware of before. In ways I know he couldn't see. It caused contemplation for myself, I wondered what can't I see? I wondered when will I be fully aware of the limits of my physical age when it comes to motherhood? When will I be able to admit my ability to have a baby is not possible anymore? In my mind and heart I still felt so young! Maybe not in my body as much, but for the moment, I still thought of myself as young enough. Just to be safe though, on my 39th birthday I asked my husband what would become an annual check-in, 'are we ready to stop trying?' We both felt convinced the answer was 'no'.

~ | | ~

It was just two days into January 2017 when recognition hit, this was the year of the milestone, and the dread kicked in. This was the year I had long ago built up in my mind as being full of obstacles to having children. At a fairly early, and naïve, age I decided that I wasn't going to be having children past forty years old. The fears I had been quieting over the last several years shifted from whisper to roar in a heartbeat. It was almost like they were getting crowded behind a door, where I had shoved them, and suddenly they sensed a weakness in the frame - probably using the same radar my bladder has, that senses when the car pulls into the driveway. They pooled their efforts and rammed the door all at once, toppling over each other as they spilled out. "What if my child resents an old mom?" "What if my old eggs cause them illness or disabilities?" "What if I am too far removed from the life of a teenager by then?" "It isn't fair to ask them to deal with aging parents at such a young age!" "They would be so young when we pass away!"

There was a moment, as I examined them all sprawled out in front of me, where I could have given in to the anxiety abyss; that hole in my chest that feels like a vacuum, which only grows hungrier the more I feed it the worries it craves. But thankfully, I was otherwise in a very good place. I drew on the counselling techniques I was both learning in school and from my personal counselor, and shoved them all back in the closet to intentionally deal with later. And made a note that door was a closet, not a garburator, like I had previously thought. It may have been easier to pack up the anxiety this time because, well, practice makes perfect, but also because of one key thing. A lesson I had not only recently been reminded of, but was about to teach a coaching workshop on. Fear is conquered by love.

Love and fear cannot share the same space, not in our hearts or minds, and not in our lives. I had been really embracing this truth the last few months, seeing how it had empowered me in my thought life, in my relationships, in my trust in God, and I knew with great certainty it was 100% true. And wherever I chose love, fears would not just get hidden in a closet, they would outright die. So I realized, I once again had a choice to make, I needed to fully embrace love if I wanted to be rid of these fears once and for all. Even if I never ended up becoming a mother, and these fears lost their power through lack of leverage, I knew they would likely be seeds for different fears one day if I didn't do something about them now. And so, I obliterated them with love.

I took the whole month of February to focus on being grateful for all the love God had poured into my life, knowing all good things come from Him. Every day I made the effort to emphasize one area of my life where His love had made a huge impact. The love He gave me for creating and setting my heart alight with our shared passion once again. The love He gave me for helping people and for filling me with His love for the hurting. The love He gave me for myself, that as He showed me who I was created to be, I was able to embrace 'me' fully. The love He surrounded me with in my friends and family, who I get to truly share life with every day. The love He gave me in my marriage, knowing He did indeed create us to be on this journey together.

Then, of course, His love for me, which He takes every opportunity to remind me of. He had relentlessly pursued my trust so that I could rest in His peace, and receive His love. I knew, if this was how much God loved me, this is how much He would love my child, and that any obstacle they faced because His timing was that they be born to old parents, He would be there to love them through it.

By the time the big day came around, I celebrated my fortieth birthday barren but with genuine joy, peace and hope. I don't have it down perfectly yet, but at least now I am able to stay anchored, not letting myself feel so stuck in the pause. In fact, for that very birthday, my husband and I got matching ring finger tattoos in the shape of anchors. Anchors add weight to a connection, they provide an unmatched depth of security in calm or rocky waters. And they are far more romantic than a ball and chain. They also remind us that with God we know we are anchored, no matter what the future holds.

~ | | ~

Back when this all started in 2010, when the fear had been in control and convinced me to quit trying to conceive, I had been working on my anxiety. I can't remember if it was suggested or I initiated it, but I was praying through Scripture, and I came across verses that said, "Rejoice always....give thanks in all circumstances." At that time I really struggled to believe I could ever be in a place of rejoicing and gratitude without being a mother. Then, several years later, with renewed hope, faith, and love, suddenly people kept telling me that the first word that came to mind when they thought of me was joy. I was, and still am, working hard to trust and depend on God every day, to stay anchored in His truth and purposes, so I was a little perplexed people could see the joy so evidently in me. Then I heard about a Greek word study for joy and found out it means 'an awareness of God's grace', and that made so much more sense. That was true joy, a peace-filled, unshakable confidence, because my dependence on God was a daily recognition of His grace in my life. And so it seems I did learn how to 'rejoice always' after all.

Epilogue

~ ~ ~

While I am still in the pregnant pause, still hoping, I am not wasting the waiting. Since 2014 I have been working to develop a support network and infertility coaching business, both online and in my local area, to help other women who find themselves stuck in the pause, looking for that elusive joy. This book is just one way I am able to pass on the gift of hope and positivity that I have found, an opportunity I am so grateful for, as well as amazed by. One of my childhood dreams was to become an author. I have been imagining stories for almost as long as I have been dreaming of being a mother. But I never dreamed that my first book would be my own story about not being a mom. Even ten years ago, when I felt God encourage my cathartic blog writing, hinting that writing was a significant part of my purpose, I couldn't have imagined the impact my story could have on others. I am blessed every day I wake up, looking forward to how my story can help one more person find a joy-ful-filled life!

While my career in infertility coaching and counselling is only getting started, I have so many other dreams for this path that are also beginning to blossom. The puzzle pieces I have felt fall into place are beginning to merge in the middle. Here I am finding, in addition to walking alongside women in a listening capacity, I can also help them convey their emotions in a creative expression, through art. And the heart my husband and I have had to strengthen marriages could one day evolve into a way we can help restore the union of those couples battered by the infertility storms. I could not be any more excited or hopeful for our future. It's hard to even imagine that place I was stuck in, when I believed infertility was the sum of my whole story, but now I know it was only a chapter. And I know there are others who still feel that way, whom I long to share hope with.

In the last four years, with even part-time exposure to this path, I have already had the privilege of witnessing the stories of so many others stuck in this same waiting room. Their pause on pregnancy is for countless different reasons, and each and every story of theirs is unique. No matter what our paused path looks like, we all share the heartbreak of hope deferred. Since I've acknowledged my own infertility, I've realized there are more of us than the statistics represent. There are so many women I want to help find hope.

Yet, hope deferred is also a universal story. We all have something that tries to rob of us of our hope. Our joy. As I've shared my journey with friends, they have shared with me that my ability to stay hopeful, after all this time, inspires them to believe for their own miracles, whatever that means to them. Sometimes we just need to see that someone has done it before us, that joy can be found despite adversity. That hope can be powerful enough to help us start the journey.

This is my story.

But it can be anyone's story.

Even yours.

~ | | ~

So, if you started reading this book in the same place of negativity and hopelessness that I did, I want to encourage you, this is only a chapter, not your entire story. And the next page you turn over is blank, yours to write on. I want you to know that your story will leave a legacy, with or without a child, and you have the ability to shape that legacy starting today.

The key is to start at the source. The source of who we are and the source of limitless hope. The source of saving grace and unshakable joy. The source of life and the meaning of it. He is waiting for you to find your everything in Him. The questions I asked God were not magic, the power lies in the fact I asked them at all. Just start with the question burning in your soul right now.

If you want to know how God feels about you, ask! If you want to know what God created you for, ask! If you want to know what you are supposed to do next, ask!

Whatever you do, just start.

If the chapter that you are in right now has made it hard to talk to God, or hear from God, ask for help. From your spouse, from a friend, from a pastor, from me.

Yes me! I would be honored to sit across a table from you, or connect across the world, and listen to your story. To share our hearts, and our heartaches. To walk alongside you as you start your own path to positivity when all the results are negative.

Whatever you do, just start.

My heart is out on the rocky seas
      of grief
Tossed around by all that stirs
      in the deep
            dark waters around me
Waves of depression and anxiety
      wash over me
          cover me
I can't breathe
Dazed I flounder
Where am I?

Hope floats by
      a life preserver
          my head now above water
But I still drift
      still wander
And then I find you
      my anchor
The storm still swirls around me
Mercilessly blowing me to and fro
      but you won't let me go
         bound to me
            you ground me
I am not lost anymore.

epilogue

Working through it

a guide book

Chapter one

~ ~ ~

"Over the years I began to feel empty and hopeless when I didn't have that thing that told me my life had meaning."

~ ~ ~

Can you identify with this feeling of hopelessness? How do you think your journey this far has contributed to feeling hopeless?

Why is reaching motherhood so important to you?

When you imagine your ideal future, what story do you tell yourself?

What are some things, which have been essential to you, that have been set aside because this dream has been a priority?

Where do you see God in your struggles right now?

Take some space to journal about what feelings this chapter brought up for you.

The Pregnant Pause

Chapter two

~ ~ ~

"While I only had a slight inclination at the time of where my motherhood journey was leading me, I had become very aware of how isolated the experience would be."

~ ~ ~

Are you keeping your struggle a secret from people? What are some reasons you are hiding what you are going through?

Who have you been able to talk to about the struggles you are experiencing? Has it been helpful to share with them?

When would you consider asking for external help to deal with, and process, the various emotions and stresses of your circumstances?

How have you and your partner been handling the decision making that comes with fertility frustrations? If you disagree, what steps are you taking to get on the same page?

How has your connection to God been throughout this journey?

Take some space to journal about what feelings this chapter brought up for you.

Chapter three

~ ~ ~

"When there is no movement being made, hope can be tremendously weighty."

~ ~ ~

Where do you feel the most weighed down, the most burdened? Your body, heart or mind? Why is that?

What are some things that people say that either hurt or help your hope?

Have you been seeking out stories similar to your own to help with the weight of hopelessness? Which ones have helped?

Describe how you feel stuck, unable to move forward in this season.

When was that last time you asked God to direct your hope?

Take some space to journal about what feelings this chapter brought up for you.

Chapter four

~ ~ ~

"The time had come to realize that the plan I was designed for was already in play.... My purpose is my purpose and that would never change, because parenthood was a circumstance not a destiny."

~ ~ ~

How does that statement make you feel? That parenthood is not a destiny. That your purpose exists regardless.

Have you reached the point when you ask, 'what now'?
Where has this question led you?

When have you said 'no' to yourself because you
prioritized motherhood? Make a list and circle the ones
where you still feel the tug of wanting to say 'yes'.

What are some hints you've received as to your potential purposes? What are three things that you get very passionate about when you talk about them?

One really helpful question you can ask God is 'what were You thinking when You created me?'

I was inspired to ask this question after watching the following video, and it was the single most important question I have ever asked God. His answer changed my life. I would encourage you to watch the video and then ask God this question for yourself, and journal about the experience.

https://youtu.be/2xDst5GDVug (particularly minutes 27 to 42)

Take some space to journal about what feelings this chapter brought up for you. Or to record your experiences with asking God this question.

The Pregnant Pause

Chapter five

~ ~ ~

"It is I who is in a box, with limits on my understanding and reach and power, not God."

~ ~ ~

How might you be 'living by sight' verses 'living by faith'?

What are the doubts about God that keep you from trusting Him completely?

Who are one or two safe people you can share your doubts about God with? Have you?

What limits might you be placing on God during this struggle?

Listening Prayer - This type of prayer is simply spending time talking to God, asking questions, and then taking time to listen to His response. God is calling us into a relationship, and relationships include two-way conversation. The Bible tells us over and over, God says 'listen for My voice.'

Begin with any burning questions, or the ones on these pages. Then give Him the space to respond, which means giving Him space to answer in His timing, but also in His own way, He might respond in a way we don't expect. It is beneficial to have a journal on hand when entering into intentional listening prayer, so you can capture the nudges, pictures, words, etc. that come to mind as He responds.

You can find more information in the book "Can You Hear Me" by Brad Jersak

Take some space to journal about what feelings this chapter brought up for you. Or to record your experiences with listening prayer.

The Pregnant Pause

Chapter six

~ ~ ~

"I thought somehow that (the break) would lighten the burden on both of us. That instantly the obstacle separating us would simply disappear. That was not the case."

~ ~ ~

What expectations do you have of your spouse that are not being met?

Men and women carry the weight of infertility differently, have you asked your spouse what it is that burdens them the most? Do you know how you are able to support them?

Is there a couple whom you admire? When you look at their marriage you think 'couple goals'? List some things about their marriage you wish for your own marriage.

Whether or not you are both on the same page about the path to parenthood, what are you doing to stay on the same page about your marriage?

Take some time over the next week to pray over what you've shared on these pages. Lift your unmet needs to God. Submit your expectations to God and try to align your plans with His. Ask God how you can be the spouse your partner needs during this season. Pray for protection of your marriage, and strength to choose each other every day. Ask God to bring you into relationship with a couple who can mentor you. Find your worth and love in Him first and foremost.

Take some space to journal about what feelings this chapter brought up for you, or write out your prayers for your marriage.

Chapter seven

~ ~ ~

"God doesn't change His original design in us. However, our perception of what that means....might be different than God's."

~ ~ ~

What are some things you feel you have lost due to infertility? How have you grieved them?

What other areas of life have been put on pause as you've addressed your fertility?

When going through health assessments and/or treatment, did you become more aware of your health and well-being? How have you acted on improving your well-being?

Is there a question you fear asking God? What answer are you afraid to receive? What would receiving that answer mean?

What other positive discoveries have you made as you have gone through these challenges?

Take some space to journal about what feelings this chapter brought up for you.

Chapter eight

~ ~ ~

"Too often, we don't turn to the one who planted the dream. Instead...our minds will create a scenario where suddenly we have the answer. We know a way that we are certain will make our dreams happen."

~ ~ ~

Sometimes our dreams for our children are rooted in unmet childhood dreams of our own? Reflect on and respond to that.

How is your purpose like a puzzle? Do you seem to have random pieces that don't connect yet? Or do you have a corner that gives a small glimpse of the big picture?

In what ways might God have been giving you what you need (not want) during this pause?

Nothing is insignificant, God likes to use everything and waste nothing. What seemingly insignificant moments have you been unable to shake? What idea keeps coming back to your mind over and over?

God never takes any dream away and leaves us empty handed, He is always wanting to place a better dream in our hearts. Have you asked Him what that looks like in your life?

Take some space to journal about what feelings this chapter brought up for you.

The Pregnant Pause

Chapter nine

~ ~ ~

"Those moments won't always look like a typical blessing, but that doesn't lessen the healing and joy I can receive from them, if I will only recognize them for what they are."

~ ~ ~

How might fear be robbing you of the hope and joy you could have?

What blessings night you be overlooking because you are comparing with someone else's?

Do you believe it is possible for you to get to a place where you can have joy in all circumstances? Why or why not?

Mindfulness – this inner practice is simply being aware of the present moment and experiencing it without judgement. Some of its benefits are:
1. Decrease depressive and anxiety symptoms
2. Decrease stress response
3. Increase self-compassion
4. Decrease symptoms of chronic or critical illnesses
5. Improves general health; lowering blood pressure, cardiovascular health, eating behaviours.
6. Improves patience and decreases reactivity
7. Enhances emotional regulation

10 Things mindful people do differently:
1. They don't believe their thoughts/feelings as facts
2. They don't try to avoid or deny their emotions
3. They understand things change, nothing stays the same forever
4. They find perspective, while realistic they choose to think on best-case not worst-case scenarios
5. They let themselves enjoy good moments thoroughly
6. They practice curiosity about life, look at it through fresh eyes
7. They slow down and take their time, giving space to not have to rush
8. They value the good things they have right now
9. They take care of their whole selves; body, mind, soul
10. They are able to laugh at themselves

For more information on this topic, please see my blog at prismpersonalcoaching.blogspot.com/p/mindfulnessarchives.html

Philippians 4:6-7 (NLT) says "Don't worry about anything; instead, pray about everything. Tell God what you need, and thank Him for all He has done. Then you will experience God's peace, which exceeds anything we can understand."

What hope do you find in this verse?

Take some space to journal about what feelings this chapter brought up for you.

Acknowledgements

First and foremost, I want to thank Jesus, my rescuer, my anchor. I could never have found my way without You. Without You, there is no way to find.

~ | | ~

Thank you so much to my husband Sean, the one who suffered and celebrated alongside me all these years. The one whose insight and support in bringing our story to life was as invaluable as it has been while living the story.

~ | | ~

Thank you also to my friends and family who encouraged me to share this story, who helped me brave the world of book publishing because of their belief in me. Specifically I would like to thank the following friends for being my advanced readers and helping me share the best version of this manuscript; Yasemee, Tami, Pamela, Megan and Roxy.

~ | | ~

And last, but not least, I want to thank my mom and dad, and all my spiritual mentors who have instilled in me a deep desire to know my Creator, the source of my everything.

References

Chapter 4

Excerpt from this blog dated January 12, 2011
http://meettheblochers.blogspot.com/2011/01/and-all-of-sudden-when-you-least-expect.html

Avicii, Lyrics to "Wake Me Up". Genius, 2018,
genius.com/Avicii-wake-me-up-lyrics

Bugbee, Bruce. "Network". Zondervan, 2004

MBTI Assessment, mbtionline.com, 2010,
mbtionline.com/TaketheMBTI

Rohr, Richard. Enneagram: "A Christian Perspective". The Crossroad Publishing Company, 2001

Cloud, Henry. "Changes That Heal". Zondervan, 1996

Chapter 5

Thomas, Gary. "Sacred Pathways: Discover Your Soul's Path to God". Zondervan, 2010

Michelle Obama. Excerpt from this video dated November 15, 2018 https://www.youtube.com/watch?v=lDxC1DBWqkc

Chapter 7

Ortberg, John. "The Me I Want to Be". Zondervan, 2009

Chapter 8

Coldplay, Lyrics to "A Sky Full of Stars". Genius, 2018,
genius.com/Coldplay-a-sky-full-of-stars-lyrics

Disney, Lyrics to "Somewhere Out There". LetsSingIt, 2018,
letssingit.com/disney-lyrics-somewhere-out-there-sp58z4f

Workbook

Walker-Smith, Kim. Excerpt from this video dated March 7, 2013 https://youtu.be/2xDst5GDVug

Jersak, Brad. "Can You Hear Me". Trafford Publishing 2003

About the Author

A lifelong writer, Lori has captured her imagination and emotions in the language of story and poetry since grade school. The last ten years Lori has used her personal blog as a way to cathartically express her struggles and insights to others also in the pregnant pause. On her journey, Lori discovered her heart for encouraging others, using her voice to acknowledge the pain of infertility, and began offering in-person and online support for other women experiencing frustration with their fertility.

While Lori continues to wait out the pregnant pause, in the meantime she finds joy being a personal life coach, expressing herself through artistic creations, and sharing life with loved ones. Lori and her husband Sean spend their short summers in Winnipeg enjoying nature, and their long winters hibernating with their cat Tubby, watching psychological thrillers.

You can find Lori at:

thepregnantpausecoach.com

pregnantpausecoaching@gmail.com

@the_pregnant_pause

If this story has moved you, please consider leaving a review at Amazon or McNally Robinson Booksellers, or dropping me a line, I would love to hear your story and how this book has impacted you! But even more valuable would be to share this book with a woman who is in the pregnant pause and needs to hear a story of hope. Thank you in advance.

Love Lori